Unbuilt Bristol

The city that might have been

1750-2050

Unbuilt Bristol
The city that might have been
1750-2050

Eugene Byrne

 redcliffe

First published in 2013 by Redcliffe Press Ltd.,
81g Pembroke Road, Bristol BS8 3EA
www.redcliffepress.co.uk
info@redcliffepress.co.uk

ISBN 978-1-908326-27-0

British Library Cataloguing-in-Publication Data
A catalogue record for this book is available from the British Library.

Design and typesetting by Stephen Morris www.stephen-morris.co.uk
set in Garamond 11.5/10
Printed and bound by Short Run Press Ltd, Exeter

Contents

7 Introduction: Paths Not Taken

12 A Bridge across the Avon Gorge (1)

14 Building Mania

16 A Bridge across the Avon Gorge (2)

21 A Garden Cemetery, Stokes Croft

23 Railway Mania (1)

24 High Cross

26 Severn Barrage

27 Pro-Cathedral

34 Dockisation of the Avon

38 Bristol Central Railway Station

39 Railway Mania (2)

40 Bristol Assize Court

42 Tidal energy from the Avon

43 Challenging the Great Western (1)

44 Tramways Terminus

46 Oatley Department Store

47 The Wrong Choice?

48 Challenging the Great Western (2)

49 Clifton Arcade

51 War Memorial

54 King George V Memorial

56 QEH Kingsweston

57 Replanning Bristol

65 Broadmead

67 The Council House Nudes

69 What shall we do about Castle Park?

71 The Dutch House

73 The City of Frampton Cotterell

74 Pathways in the Air

77 Central Telephone Exchange

78 The Grand Spa Hotel

80 Filling in the Docks

85 Bristol & West Tower

87 20 Ideas for Bristol

89 Blue Wave

91 200 Ideas for Bristol

94 The Avon Metro (and its descendants)

98 Football Grounds

100 Avon Weir

104 Harbourside Centre

108 The People's Cultural Palace

110 The Orbit Millennium Project

113 Wingbridge

114 Bristol Venice/Little Venice

115 The Bristol Pyramid (now The Pyramid)

117 Bristol Arena

120 Museum of Bristol

121 The St Paul's Tower

123 The Chocolate Factory and Cycle Houses

125 Afterword: A Transatlantic Tunnel, Hurrah!

128 Acknowledgements

Paths Not Taken

Imagine a woman. For the sake of argument we'll call her Sarah and say that she lives in Birmingham.

Imagine the year is now, that it's a lovely day, and that Sarah got up early this morning to catch a train from New Street station to Bristol.

Sarah is in her thirties, has a degree in whatever subject you fancy and lives with her partner (make up your own name for him here) and their son Tom, who has just started primary school. Sarah has a full-time job with a housing association, and she's coming to Bristol for a conference.

She's going to be away from home for three days and two nights. She's going to miss Tom and What's-His-Name, of course, but looks on this as a small and well-deserved almost-holiday, a break from the full-time job, from looking after a bright and energetic five-year-old and doing more than her fair share of the housework.

She's quite excited about the conference; there are some interesting-looking speakers and panel discussions, and she'll see some old friends and former colleagues. She's also keen to get a look around Bristol. Everyone's always going on about what a great place it is.

The train is about to pull into Bristol's Queen Square station.

Sarah folds the free copy of the *Daily Herald* that British Rail passengers are given. She smiles again at the cartoon on the front page. President Blair is on a state visit to France where last night he was treated to a lavish banquet at Versailles hosted by King Louis XXI. The cartoonist has drawn the French King and Prime Minister Depardieu grovelling to Blair, who is seated on a throne. After years of trying to go it alone, and pretending they were still a great power, the French are now desperate to join the Euro. President Blair has enough clout to be able to swing it for them.

Ah, yes. You see, our imaginary Sarah lives in a parallel universe. It's a world like our own in all its essentials, but here history has worked out differently. At some point in the past, the respective timelines of Sarah's world and ours diverged.

Sarah wonders whether she should take a cab to her hotel straight away, or if she should do a little sight-seeing first. The conference doesn't begin until this afternoon. She gets off the train and wheels her suitcase along the platform towards the main exit. Stopping to check the big you-are-here map she sees she's just a short walk from the city centre. Little symbols on it also show the Avon Metro stops.

It's such a nice morning that she decides she'll walk for a while, and then take one of the trams to the hotel. Out in the sunshine, she admires the Bath stone masonry of the station, all elaborate and sort of Victorian Gothic. People say it was built by Brunel, but she's not sure. People say everything Victorian in

Bristol was built by Brunel.

This is the first time she's seen the middle of Bristol in daylight. She's passed through a few times before, and there was one particularly debauched weekend here years ago when she was a student and visiting friends. Though that was mostly spent in the clubs and bars along the city's legendary Castle Street party zone.

She decides she approves. The Centre is almost completely free of traffic, there's a nice mish-mash of architecture here, and a quite pleasant landscaped garden that runs through the middle of it, though it does have the look of an old municipal park.

She passes a weird column at the top of the old harbour. She stops to read. It's dedicated to the memory of His Late Majesty King George V. He was the one with the beard, wasn't he? Maybe he had some important connection with Bristol.

Walking along the pavement and following the tramlines in the road she's soon in a large green area with a big semicircular building at the top. The town hall. She recognises it from photos on various documents and articles she's read about local government down the years.

There's a tram-stop next to a big church – the cathedral? – and she decides she'll go on to the hotel now. Her shoes aren't sensible enough for too much walking while also lugging a suitcase.

'Line 2, N', she wrote on her wrist at 6.30 this morning. Yes, this is the right stop. The electronic timetable tells her that the next tram will be along in two minutes, giving her plenty of time to admire (if that's the word) the statue at this end of the Council HQ. A huge bronze figure of a naked woman holding up her fingers and kicking out one leg to the side.

She wonders if Bristolians love this bizarre thing, or if it's an object of ridicule.

The tram pulls up. It's red, surprisingly dirty and old-fashioned looking, and apparently with no elect-ronic payment facilities. She has to hand the driver cash for her fare. Lack of investment, she thinks to herself primly.

She finds a seat. The map overhead says she's six stops from her destination. She pulls some papers from the pocket at the front of her case.

The conference opens at 2pm with coffee and a brief welcome speech from the Lord Mayor. The first talk is all about housing issues in Bristol, and how building a weir across the river somewhere back in the 1990s turned a load of former industrial land and canals full of shopping trolleys into prime develop-ment sites for public and private housing. Might be interesting, she thinks.

Over to her left, she can now see more of the old Harbour, and Brunel's ship, the ss *Great Britain*, now restored and a huge tourist attraction.

One of the options on the social programme for this evening is a tour of the Stokes Croft Necropolis, a huge big Victorian cemetery not far from the city centre. There was a time when it was owned by a private company, which wanted to turn it all into housing and offices, but a campaign by local people put a stop to that, and now it's run as a sort of living museum and wildlife reserve.

Clifton Rocks Railway is the next stop. Hers. She puts the papers away and pushes the bell.

She knows what to do here. The instructions came with her hotel booking.

She gets out. Oh. Wow. There it is!

The Avon Bridge itself. 'Vicksville', the locals call it. Vick for the man who paid for it, and ville because, well, it's a small town all on its own. Grade I listed building, subject of countless paintings, chocolate boxes, jigsaws, postcards ... The vast, ornate eighteenth-century bridge across the gorge; there was a time when people lived in it, though nowadays it's an upmarket mall ... Louis Vuitton, Burberry, Christian Louboutin, Prada, and all sorts of jewellers, and tiny shops where an even tinier box of chocolates will cost you a hundred Euro.

Sarah would not be at all surprised if Bristolians moaned about how their city's most iconic building, a priceless piece of their heritage, England's own Ponte Vecchio, has been turned over to selling overpriced tat to the rich and stupid. But then again ... There'd be no harm in wandering over to take a look if there's time...

According to the instructions from the hotel, the easiest thing to do is now cross the road.

As she waits for the crossing light to change, she notices the Avon View Hotel for the first time. It had been hard to spot before, not just because of the way the bridge grabs your attention, but because it appears to have been camouflaged.

She knows all about this. Asif, her boss at work, comes from Bristol and explained his sense of mixed-up jealousy and outrage when she said she'd be staying at the Avon View. Back when it was built in the 1970s, he said, Bristolians were appalled that this massive concrete monstrosity was being stuck on the side of the Gorge.

'It was a horrible eyesore,' he said. 'It ruined the natural beauty of the Gorge, and it looked shabby next to the bridge. People have been demanding it be pulled down ever since. But you might as well stay there, because it means you won't have to look at it from the outside.'

At some point in the last few years, the Hotel's owners had the bright idea of cladding it in huge sheets of green, grey and blue-tinted glass to give it a sort of camouflage effect. She is not at all sure that this works.

At the entrance to the Clifton Rocks Railway, she fumbles around in her purse for a Euro coin to get through the turnstile.

'Let me help you with that,' says an extremely well-spoken old gentleman looking very smart in a black uniform, complete with peaked cap, as he takes her case and puts it into the car. He then holds the door open for her as she gets in. The rush hour has been and gone, and she's the only passenger.

The man smiles, and returns to a little kiosk in front of the car. The doors close, and it begins its journey up through a tunnel cut out of the rocks. Behind his glass panel, the man nods and smiles at her. She wonders if he's staff or a volunteer.

The car moves slowly up through the tunnel. Good job I'm not claustrophobic, she thinks to herself. A notice over her head answers her earlier question. 'The Clifton Rocks Funicular Railway was brought back into operation by volunteers, and is run by volunteers. If you value it, please feel free to make a donation. There are collection boxes at the top and bottom.'

Ten minutes later, Sarah is in her hotel room. No, of course it wouldn't be a room with spectacular views of the Gorge and bridge. Even though she's here off-season, and even though the conference has negotiated a special deal with the hotel for its attendees, this is still a five-star hotel where the rooms with the best views are prohibitively expensive.

Later on, she will take the Metro tram back down town to the conference at the People's Cultural Palace, down on the Harbourside. That was something else that got old Asif all excited. 'It is an amazing building, Sarah! I promise you that you will absolutely love it. Much of it was built by volunteers as a multi-faith centre, concert hall and conference centre. You cannot imagine what a strange mixture of styles it is.'

But first, time to freshen up, then get a cup of coffee, and then just the short walk over to look at the Avon Bridge, and be shocked at the prices of everything in the shops on it. After all, it would be silly not to visit it if you're only staying a few hundred yards away.

* * * * *

That was just a bit of fun, but you get the idea. In her parallel universe, Sarah has just encountered a number of things which were going to be built in Bristol at one time or another.

Science fiction and fantasy writers call this sort of thing 'alternate history' and have been doing it for decades. Historians only discovered the concept more recently; some treat it with disdain, while others will play it as a sort of parlour game and call it 'counterfactual history'.

It has its uses. If you are trying to construct a counterfactual story, one of the first things you discover is that it's harder than you expect. In real history, things have a habit of happening because they are supposed to. There are social, economic, political, cultural and other forces at work which make things turn out the way they do. A lot of history happens because of accidents, fortuitous or unfortunate events, battles won or lost, but most of history happens because broad forces dictate how things are meant to happen.

This is a book about just a few of the structures which might have been built in Bristol over the last 250 or so years. It doesn't pretend to be comprehensive; there are plenty of other schemes which didn't merit the space, or have been completely forgotten. There will also certainly be some which have been missed out through my own negligence.

(Sharp-eyed readers will also notice that despite the book's title, the earliest date here is 1764, not 1750. But 1750 is a nice round figure. If you want unbuilt projects from 1750 and earlier then look into all the ancient proposals to improve Bristol's port, or create a 'floating harbour'.)

The schemes that do feature here range from the extremely fanciful and unrealistic through to the hard-headed and relentlessly commercial. The only thing they all have in common is that they never happened, or that they did happen, only in a different form.

If you were to try and create a much larger alternate history of Bristol using some of them, if you were to try and write a bigger, longer story than that of Sarah's arrival, you would very quickly run into huge problems making your story stand up. Even in the short tale above, it seemed necessary to use a little artistic licence. Like that stuff about camouflage glass cladding on a hotel which would have been (according to its critics) hideous. Or, more culpably, claiming that the Avon Metro would have run out along the Portway when no such line was ever proposed; it would have gone up through Clifton. And obviously the re-opening of the Clifton Rocks funicular railway is something we all hope will happen one day.

Most of these unbuilt projects failed for reasons which were good or bad, but which most of the time were strong reasons. Taken together, they form a useful alternative way of looking at the history of Bristol over the last 250 years. They tell us a very great deal about the priorities and problems of the city (or, more specifically, of its ruling elite) over time. One cannot fail to be struck, for instance, by the way in which conservation of the environment or of old buildings, is something nobody cared much about until the late twentieth century. Or take the breath-taking and visionary scale of the ambitions of those planning to rebuild Bristol at the end of the Second World War, or the whole story of Bristol's desperate attempts to deal with its traffic and transport problems – which begin a lot sooner than you might expect.

On a less intellectual level, almost all of them are just amusing or interesting to look at in their own right. Apart, that is, from all the football-ground plans, and the dreary saga of tram and light rail schemes. Those are just confusing.

A Bridge across the Avon Gorge (1) 1764-1793

Mr. William Vick, a wealthy wine merchant, residing in Queen Square ... died on the 3rd January, 1764. By his will, Mr. Vick, after sundry dispositions, left his residuary estate to his sister Rebecca and to Roger Watts, subject to the payment of £1,000 to the Merchants' Society, directing that this sum should be invested, together with the yearly interest, until it should have accumulated to £10,000. When that sum had been attained, the Society were directed to construct a stone bridge over the Avon from Clifton Down to the opposite height, the passage to be free from toll ... The terms of Mr. Vick's bequest appear to have excited as much amusement as surprise, and witless gibes at the old wine merchant's morality have been re-echoed in our own time.

John Latimer, *The Annals of Bristol in the Eighteenth Century* (1893)

The very idea of a bridge across the Avon Gorge started out as the whim of a rich merchant, and, as Latimer attested, it excited a great deal of ridicule.

The engineering know-how for spanning the wide and deep Avon Gorge did not exist in Vick's time. And why build a bridge anyway? In 1764 and for a long time afterwards, there was no pressing need for it. Very few people lived on either side of its projected location – most of Clifton had not been built yet – and it was not on any major routes to anywhere.

By the late 1700s the idea was a little less ridiculous. There was a building boom in progress, and those who could afford it were moving away from the noise, smells and overcrowding of central Bristol to the airy new suburb of Clifton.

In 1793, William Bridges published a truly spectacular plan reflecting the boundless confidence of the time. Had Bridges' design ever been built, and had it survived to the present day, it would now be one of the world's most recognisable structures.

Bridges' bridge would act as an impressive entrance portal to the city and harbour of Bristol. The huge arch would be 220ft high and 180ft wide, more than adequate for the largest vessels of its day, and certain to be approved by the Admiralty, which had the power of veto over any structure that might impede the movement of naval vessels.

Bridges' plan was also old-fashioned, looking back to the medieval practice of putting businesses on bridges – as, for example, with the old Bristol Bridge.

Its five storeys would be served by lifts. The abutment on the Clifton side would contain granaries, a corn exchange and even a chapel. There would also be a coal wharf to satisfy the huge demand for coal from all the big new houses in Clifton. The abutment on the Leigh Woods side would contain factories, a naval school and a library.

Tellingly, there would also be a stone wharf, because Bridges anticipated that once the bridge was built, a huge uninhabited stretch of countryside around Leigh Woods would be ripe for building development.

Not long after Bridges published his plan, war broke out with France. This, and the end of the Clifton building boom, put a stop to Bridges'

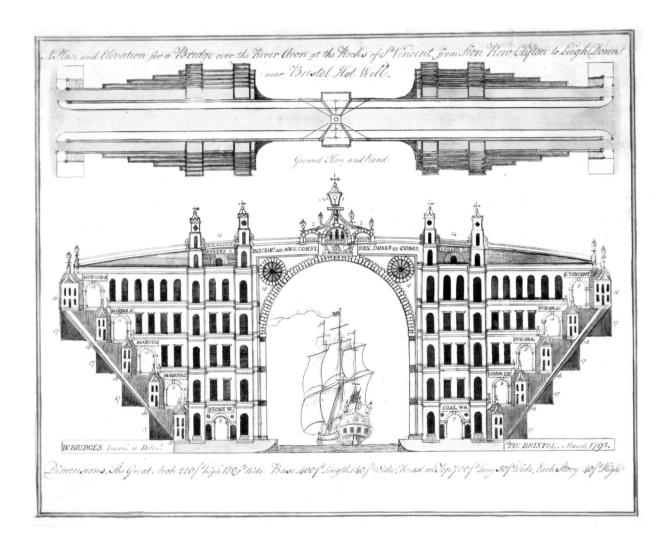

ambitions. A bridge over the Gorge wouldn't be discussed again for a generation.

William Bridges. *Design for a bridge over the Avon at Clifton, Bristol*, 1793. (RIBA Library Drawings & Archives Collections)

Building Mania 1786-1793

In the late 1700s, Bristol's population and economy were growing rapidly, much of this because of the huge profits being made from Bristol's trading connections with the sugar plantations in the West Indies. Of course the basis of much of Bristol's growing wealth was slave labour.

By the mid-1780s a speculative housing boom was under way to the north and west of the city. Whole streets and terraces were being built in Clifton (Sion Row, around Brandon Hill, Great George Street, Park Street) and other suburban areas (Portland Square and Kingsdown, for example).

In 1791 a local newspaper noted:

So great is the spirit of building in this city and its environs that we hear ground is actually taken for more than 3,000 houses, which will require some hundreds more artificers than are already employed.

These developments included streets which would eventually be built, such as Royal York and Cornwallis Crescents, as well as developments which would not. When Thomas Tyndall, owner of the Royal Fort house and its surrounding parkland, died in 1790, a group of businessmen bought the land – they reportedly paid £40,000 for it – with a view to building houses over the entire 68-acre site. There was going to be a huge terrace of smart homes here.

The standard version of the story goes that when war broke out with Revolutionary France in 1793, these and several other schemes – including plans for houses on Clifton Down and Ashley Down – all collapsed in the ensuing financial crisis. If you look at it closely, however, it's clear that even without war this was a bubble which would burst sooner or later anyway. The Royal York Crescent scheme, for example, was in trouble before the war had started.

When war came, builders great and small were ruined. Over 60 would be bankrupted in the coming years and for most of the rest of the 1790s and beyond several houses were left half-built in Royal York Crescent, Cornwallis Crescent, The Mall, Richmond Place, Kingsdown and St Michaels Hill and several other places.

Many of these houses would eventually be completed as originally designed, while others were finished in modified (usually smaller) form. If you walk along Windsor Terrace, for instance, you can see how two of the houses in the centre were completed (by 1792) to the original design, thought to be by John Eveleigh of Bath. The rest of the houses, smaller and less ornamented, were finished in the early 1800s. This, however, would be only half of the terrace that was initially proposed – see illustration opposite.

Windsor Terrace is, if you like, the greatest monument to the building bubble of the 1780s/90s. 'Its rampant disorder,' says the Bristol Pevsner Guide, '... is an object lesson in how not to build a terrace.' It is a sign of the speculative mania of the time that it was built at all; on the side of a hill, it required a massive and hugely expensive 70ft-high abutment to support it. This fortress-like structure, still visible to this day, consumed the entire fortune which Redcliffe plumber William Watts had made from patenting his new method of making lead shot. The half-built site was

put up for sale in 1792, and Watts himself was declared bankrupt two years later.

The Tyndalls Park scheme had collapsed completely by then, with only some foundations laid. The Tyndall family would regain ownership of the site a few years later.

▲

Proposals for the development of Clifton, c.1787. This drawing by architectural surveyor and draughtsman James Blackamore may have been made for Bath architect John Eveleigh. The design for Windsor Terrace, only half of which would be built, bears a strong resemblance to Eveleigh's Camden Terrace in Bath. (By permission of Francis Greenacre)

A Bridge across the Avon Gorge (2) 1829-1864

By the time the Avon bridge was back on the agenda, a lot had changed. One of the revolutions brought about by the steam engine was not that the ships could necessarily run faster, but they could run more reliably as they weren't dependent on the winds. There was talk of a regular mail service to Ireland, running from somewhere near the mouth of the Avon on the Somerset side (so that it did not have to come all the way into Bristol along the twisting – and tidal – river). This would require a fast road link from Bristol, and a bridge over the Avon would speed things along nicely.

Another important technological development had taken place; iron bridges could be built far more cheaply than stone ones. Thomas Telford's Menai Suspension Bridge opened in 1826 and spanned 577ft. It was profitable, and attracted huge numbers

Thomas Telford's design for a suspension bridge across the River Avon. (By courtesy of the Brunel Institute – a collaboration of the ss *Great Britain* Trust and the University of Bristol)

of sightseers.

Meanwhile, William Vick's £1,000 legacy from 1764 had now grown to £8,000. If a stone bridge over the Avon was expensive and impractical, one of the new suspension bridges might not be. A committee of influential citizens was formed including the mayor, the president of the Chamber of Commerce, members of the Corporation and the Society of Merchant Venturers. An Act of Parliament was sought to gain permission for a bridge. The committee also petitioned for the condition in Vick's will that the bridge be toll-free to be overturned. Whatever was going to be built would cost considerably more than what was in Vick's pot. The lion's share of the money would have to come from donations, loans and tolls.

Meanwhile, the committee invited engineers to send in plans for what would be the highest and longest suspension bridge the world had yet seen.

One of the more spectacular concepts entered in the bridge competition: the 'romantic ruin' look was all the rage at the time. *Design for a Suspension Bridge across the River Avon*, by C.H. Capper. (By courtesy of the Brunel Institute – a collaboration of the ss *Great Britain* Trust and the University of Bristol) ▼

▲ 'Egyptian' details in Isambard Kingdom Brunel's competition drawings for the Clifton Suspension Bridge (By courtesy of the Brunel Institute – a collaboration of the ss *Great Britain* Trust and the University of Bristol)

While several plans and drawings from various people exist, it's not clear how many entries there were. There were probably more than 20, and they came from the leading engineers of the day. There was also one from the young and almost unknown Isambard Kingdom Brunel which made it to the shortlist of five finalists which the committee invited Thomas Telford to judge.

Telford rejected them all. He said Brunel's was 'pretty and ingenious' but reckoned it would collapse in a high wind. Brunel was certain that the whole Gorge could be safely spanned by a suspension bridge, but Telford was not. He ruled that none of the other designs were suitable either.

The committee now asked Telford to come up with a design of his own. Telford came back within a few weeks with one of the most bizarre proposals in all of Bristol's history. Had this structure been built, and were it still standing, it would be rather more famous than the bridge we have today.

Believing the Gorge could not safely be bridged by a single span, Telford proposed a suspension bridge supported by two massive towers. These would be ornamented in the Gothic style, making them look like freakishly elongated church towers (see illustration page 16). The committee approved Telford's design, but local opposition soon arose. Some questioned the estimated £52,000 cost of the work, while others complained that it would ruin the natural beauty of the Gorge.

Brunel was incensed and amused. In one of the best-known examples of his famous sarcasm, he wrote to the bridge committee:

As the distance between the opposite rocks was considerably less than what has always been considered as being within the limits to which suspension bridges might be carried, the idea of going to the bottom of the valley for the purpose of raising, at great expense, two intermediate supporters hardly occurred to me...what a reflection such timidity will cast on the state of the Arts today.

Thomas Telford was the elder statesman of British engineering, while Brunel was just a youthful upstart, albeit one whose father was a well-known and respected engineer. Brunel returned with a modified version of Telford's plan. There were still two immense towers, but it would be more plainly ornamented in the then-fashionable Egyptian style, and it would cost £10,000 less.

Now other designs came forward as well, many of them from local men this time around.

Parliamentary permission for the bridge was granted in May 1830, but King George IV died the following month, and all business was suspended as many of the bridge committee members were now involved in election campaigns. When they met again in October they announced a new competition. This time, it would be judged by John Seward, a London iron manufacturer and mathematician, and Davies Gilbert, a Cornish engineer and politician (he was MP for Helston) and expert on suspension bridges.

Telford's design was tactfully 'set aside' on grounds of cost. In a meeting with Gilbert, Brunel produced detailed drawings and mathematical calculations and won the day.

Gilbert did, however, require that Brunel make a lot of changes. Telford's views on the safe length of the span prevailed up to a point. It would be limited to 703ft by the building of an abutment on the Leigh Woods side. This massive brick-built structure remains to this day; it accounted for a huge chunk of the bridge budget – £14,000 – and it was not necessary.

The saga of various attempts to complete the Clifton Suspension Bridge is a long one. The project was hamstrung by financial problems, first as a result of the collapse of business confidence after the 1831 Queen Square riots, and work started and stopped again in the intervening years.

The bare towers became known to Bristolians as 'Vicksville' (after William Vick); the one on the Clifton side became a popular picnic spot. For some years an iron bar along which a large basket could travel spanned the Gorge. Originally for use by construction workers, it became a popular local white-knuckle ride.

On one occasion, it is reported, a bride and bride-groom on their wedding day resolved on taking a trip over the fragile bridge; unfortunately the hauling ropes got out of order just as they reached the middle of the bar, and they were left for some hours to discuss the beauty of the scenery... (John Latimer, *The Annals of Bristol in the Nineteenth Century*, 1897).

Brunel did not live to see the bridge completed. The bridge there nowadays is not, some contend, Brunel's design at all.

In 1860, a year after Brunel's death, John Hawk-shaw, President of the Institution of Civil Engineers and his fellow engineer William Barlow, suggested that the chains from the Hungerford Suspension Bridge, which was about to be replaced, could be used to complete the Clifton bridge. Brunel had made the Hungerford bridge and the chains were of the same design as those needed for Clifton. Hawkshaw and Barlow proposed finishing the job as a monument to their friend and colleague, Mr Brunel.

A new company was formed, money was raised, the Hungerford chains were bought and taken to Bristol on Brunel's Great Western Railway. A new Act of Parliament was secured as the old one had long-since

▲ Samuel Jackson, *View of the Avon Gorge With the Approved Design for the Clifton Suspension Bridge*, (detail) 1831 (Bristol's Museums, Galleries & Archives)

lapsed, and work began. Hawkshaw and Barlow, however, made many changes to Brunel's design. A third chain was added to the two he had specified to support additional weight. There were new anchorage pits and significantly more ironwork.

The Egyptian decorations were all gone. Brunel had also wanted to case the towers in iron, with depictions of figures engaged in the work of building the bridge; these, too, were omitted.

You could argue, then, that Brunel's Clifton Suspen-

sion Bridge is one of the greatest of all of Bristol's unbuilt structures. Brunel's own family believed the new bridge was nothing to do with the one he had designed, and so turned down their invitations to the opening ceremony.

A Garden Cemetery, Stokes Croft 1831-1839

They may have lacked our modern medical knowledge, but people in the 1830s knew well enough that cities were chronically unhealthy places – and Bristol was one of the most unhealthy of them all. A rapidly growing population of the living also meant a corresponding rise in the number of dead, and the city's old medieval churchyards could no longer cope.

This was why a huge garden cemetery was opened by a private company at Arnos Vale in 1839. After almost all Bristol's old parish graveyards were closed down on government orders in the 1850s, it would become the city's principal burial place for decades. Fashionable new garden cemeteries were all the rage at this time, opening up all over the country, particularly in big cities. Originally inspired by Père Lachaise cemetery in Paris, these were landscaped gardens, usually built in a rural or semi-rural location, away from the noise and corruption (physical and moral) of the town.

Arnos Vale cemetery did not happen overnight. The matter had been discussed for some years beforehand. This was at the same time as Bristol's new Zoological Gardens were being planned, and at one point, it looked as though the Zoo would have been built at Arnos Vale.

An alternative plan for a Bristol cemetery was put forward by a Mr P. Masey, Jr. Writing in the *Gardener's Magazine* in July 1836 he says he originally drew up his plan in 1831 but was publishing it here in the hope of drumming up some enthusiasm for the idea. The publication to which Masey submitted his article was extremely significant. The *Gardener's Magazine* was published by John Claudius Loudon (1783-1843), one of the leading botanists and garden designers of his day. He was also the most influential figure in the British garden cemetery movement.

Masey's plan was a remarkable one. After looking at various possible sites around Bristol, including Tyndall's Park and the land around Redland Parish church, he decided on a 30-acre stretch of land to the east of Stokes Croft, and north of Portland Square.

There were to be two main entrances; to the north at Wellington Place, and to the south at the northern end of Dean Street. Had it been built, it would have taken in a large part of modern St Pauls, including City Road and the surrounding streets. Given that Bristol's existing graveyards amounted to just over 15 acres combined, it would have tripled the amount of burial space in the city.

The cemetery would be extensively planted and landscaped, with a carriage road through the middle. The main pathways would serve as a public promenade for walks on Sundays and summer evenings; these would be lined with trees to offer seclusion to those wishing to visit the graves of loved ones. With its extensive and wide-ranging plantings, it would serve as a facility for those interested in botany, and there would even be a pond for aquatic plants.

There were other remarkable features; at one end would be 'a range of catacombs, built with Hanham or Stapleton stone, and cased with natural rock en masse.' Masey also designed special circular sections for the graves of people from particular fields of endeavour; there would be one for army and naval

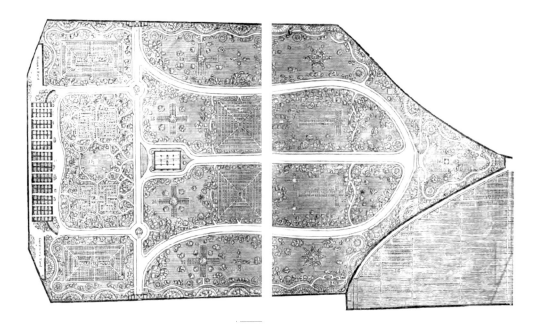

▲ Masey's plan for a garden cemetery near Stokes Croft. The main entrances are at the top and bottom on the left, while at the far left are the catacombs. The returned (or replica) Bristol High Cross would have been at the right

officers, another for 'literary characters' and a special one for local philanthropists. This latter would have 'weeping ash or willows planted in the centre, to represent the feelings of the widows and orphans they have benefited.'

There would of course have been a chapel, though no designs or plans were offered for this, but Masey envisaged a view straight down the pathway from the back of the chapel to the Bristol High Cross at the far end of the cemetery. He believed it was likely that it could be returned from Stourhead, but if this was not possible, then a replica should be built.

Of Philip Masey Junior, we know very little. Ten years previously he and his father had been partners in a business dealing in tobacco and snuff, and a subsequent letter to the *Gardener's Magazine* suggests he had some scientific knowledge, but what he did for a living remains unclear. His article makes it plain that he was a man of limited means, but that he was offering his proposal to the public in the hope that it, or something like it, would one day come to fruition. It's worth noting that in the year of publication, the Bristol General Cemetery Company, which would go on to open Arnos Vale three years later, was set up. Perhaps Masey was angling for a job as the designer. If this was the case, he was unsuccessful; Arnos Vale was laid out, and its buildings designed, by Bristol architect Charles Underwood (1791-1883).

Masey's vision, though, remains hugely attractive; it was going to be a huge necropolis, and much more besides. It would also have been a scientific study facility, arboretum and public park. With Bristol's ancient high cross in a place of honour, and its dedicated sections for memorials to local men and women of achievement, it was also to be a focus of civic pride, a place where the dead would still have been very much among the living.

Railway Mania (1) mid-1840s

When the directors of what would become the Great Western Railway Company invited a bumptious young engineer named Isambard Brunel to survey a line from Bristol to London, their ambition, which was big and expensive enough on its own, was just that – to build and operate a railway running from the city to the capital and stopping at several points in between.

Early rail pioneers imagined that the whole nation would one day be covered by a network of interconnecting railways, but it was a distant prospect. The railway system the Victorians bequeathed us is an agglomeration of routes and lines built by numerous private companies from the 1820s onwards. But for every success, there were several more companies which went bust.

The railways also triggered a succession of financial bubbles and crashes. The first and greatest speculative 'railway mania' in Britain peaked in 1845, coinciding with the opening of Bristol's very own stock exchange in April of that year. During this period around 1,000 different schemes were being proposed across the country; had they all been built, it would have been at a total cost of £700 million, an utterly unimaginable and unaffordable sum at a time when total annual spending for the UK was less than £60m.

Bristol's part in the 1840s bubble was small compared with the rest of the country, perhaps because the city was already comparatively well-served by the new Great Western and Bristol & Gloucester railways. Nonetheless some local speculators made and lost fortunes.

An anonymous author in the *Bristol Times* – almost certainly the paper's owner and editor Joseph Leech – wrote years later:

Fairy legends had no wonders for us like that time. You saw a man to-day in the streets of Bristol whom you would not trust with the loan of a five pound note; to-morrow he splashed you with the wheels of a new Long-acre carriage. He was as suddenly transformed from a twenty pound house to a mansion in the country, and though small beer refreshed him during the greater part of his life, he now became critical in the taste of Bordeaux. A railway, in fact, was not a means of transport but a thing to bet and gamble about...

Once in the height of the sorrowful farce, I had occasion to call on a couple of 'bold brokers' in a certain street not a mile from the centre of Bristol. The flavour of old Havannahs and new scrip filled the place; the clerks were having chops and tomato sauce, and a silver-necked bottle proved

HIGH CROSS

Bristol's medieval market cross stood for hundreds of years at the junction of Corn, Wine, Broad and High Streets. Back in its pomp it was richly gilded and painted, and featured little statues of kings who had done Bristol some or other favour – John, Henry III, Edward III and Edward IV. Henry VI, Elizabeth, James I and Charles I were added in the 1630s.

In the 1700s it was thought to be an obstacle to traffic and was moved to College Green, but people didn't much like it there and in 1768 it was given to Henry Hoare, who erected it at his estate at Stourhead, where it remains to this day.

Down the years the exiled Cross has become to Bristol what the Elgin Marbles are to Greece, with periodic articles and letters in the local press suggesting (or demanding) that it should be returned. When Philip Masey was proposing his garden cemetery in the 1830s, a petition had been circulating in the city for this purpose.

Bristolians 'repenting the folly of this gift' (as one commentator put it) had a replica made in the 1850s which stood on College Green once more. This was removed in the twentieth century, and all that remains of it stands in a corner of Berkeley Square in Clifton.

One of the objections to the return of the original used to be that it would survive better in the clean air of Wiltshire than in the coal- and car-exhaust-infested atmosphere of the city. There's no question that it has been well looked-after, both by the Hoare family, and the National Trust, which has owned Stourhead since 1946, but doubtless calls for its return will continue.

they enjoyed at least a reversion of the Saint Peray from the principal's apartment, into which I was summoned. Softly I trod on a Turkey carpet; a tray well furnished stood on a sideboard; and piles of prospectuses flanked the fine ponderous bronze inkstand of the man of projects, who sat in a richly cushioned chair. Voices issued from the neighbouring room, where the second principal saw others on business, and the click of plates and occasional flying of corks proved how actively the business of allotments was progressing. But they came like shadows, and so departed.

During this period private companies were formed (or mooted) for a range of schemes in and around Bristol. The more serious ones submitted bills to Parliament seeking permission to build.

These included the Dover and Bristol Railway, which would have connected Bristol to several points in the south of England, via a comparatively small line to existing or proposed lines. It seemed sensible enough for the *Iron Times* – yes, there was even a daily newspaper riding the crest of the rail boom – to editorialise: 'We ... fearlessly prognosticate success to the Dover and Bristol Railway.'

This scheme collapsed when the bubble burst amid a number of lawsuits, including a very revealing case in which an engineer claimed for unpaid wages. The court was told he was being remunerated at almost ten times the normal going rate because engineers were in such demand during the boom.

The Portbury Pier and Railway Company proposed a rail link from Bristol to Portishead via a tunnel under Failand, engineered by Brunel. Directors and shareholders baulked at the cost, and the landowner was persuaded to agree to a cutting rather than a tunnel through his land, but the scheme appears to have failed in the railway shares crash. It has been suggested that Brunel considered making this an 'atmospheric' system in which the carriages are not pulled by a locomotive, but are instead propelled by air pressure via a piston running along a pneumatic tube. Brunel would in 1847 build such a system for the South Devon Railway Company, and it was a technical and commercial disaster.

The most urgent of Bristol's rail needs was a fast connection to South Wales and its lucrative coal and iron industries. In 1845 the newly-formed Bristol and South Wales Junction Railway Company issued a prospectus calling for £200,000 in capital. This was quickly raised and the share prices rose dramatically.

The company gained the necessary Act of Parliament in 1846 to build a line from near Temple Meads to the Old Passage (near Aust) and the New Passage (near Pilning) via Baptist Mills, Horfield and Almondsbury. Brunel was hired to survey a route across the Severn, and the firm purchased the New Passage ferry. The scheme also envisaged another rail link from the northern shore of the river onwards to Chepstow and Monmouth.

To modern eyes, the scheme appears clumsy because it is not an unbroken rail link. Passengers and goods would have to be taken across the river by ferry. Nonetheless it would still have been a considerably shorter journey than the rail trip from Bristol to South Wales via Gloucester.

In fact, another company did propose a railway bridge over the Severn, and at exactly the same time.

The Bristol and Liverpool Railway Junction Company issued a prospectus proposing to raise £2 million in capital. It engaged the Gloucestershire engineer Thomas Fulljames (who also proposed the first Severn barrage) who came up with two designs for a suspension bridge across the Severn. At first the idea was widely considered absurd, but Fulljames and the company demonstrated – 120 years before an actual Severn Bridge was opened – that it was a perfectly viable proposition. The Admiralty's engineers examined the plans and gave the scheme their approval.

The railway bubble burst in the autumn of 1845. Share prices in rail companies plummeted, ruining thousands of shareholders across Britain, and making it impossible for the Bristol and Liverpool Railway Junction Company to raise the necessary capital.

The scheme limped on for some years; it spent a third of the capital it had raised, but in the new business climate found it was impossible to raise enough money to start work.

No sooner had the firm dissolved in 1853 than a new company arose. The Bristol and South Wales Union Railway, as it would later become known, was going to build a line right through the centre of Bristol and along the Avon Gorge to New Passage and a ferry. Once again, the engineering would be overseen by Brunel, and the line would have gone from Temple Meads station, through Queen Square and along to Hotwells, Sea Mills and Shirehampton. There would be a 'floating bridge' over the Severn – a ferry which would carry entire trains.

These plans ran into trouble almost at once; not enough people wanted to subscribe to shares and while Bristol's Corporation approved, it was likely to encounter opposition from those who didn't want a railway running close to their homes and businesses.

Not long afterwards, a second, cheaper plan was adopted, Parliamentary approval was secured and work began in 1858, only this time the route was to the east and north of the city, complete with intermediate stations at Lawrence Hill, Stapleton Road, Filton, Patchway and Pilning – some of which are still in use to this day. Following Brunel's death in 1859 the engineering works were completed by Robert Pearson Brereton. There was no 'floating bridge', just a ferry.

Severn Barrage 1849-present

Strictly speaking, a Severn barrage shouldn't feature in a book about unbuilt developments in Bristol, but the idea of harnessing the massive tidal range of the Severn to generate power is one which has had a powerful grip on the city and surrounding areas – indeed, the whole country – for a very long time.

A barrier across the Severn, or even in the Bristol Channel, has been seriously discussed for over 150 years. There is even a bizarre legend, popular on both English and Welsh sides of the water, that one of the things Hitler would have done following a successful German occupation of Britain would be to order its construction, presumably using forced labour. Unless someone can come up with some firm evidence of this, it has to remain a legend. One suspects that neither Hitler nor any of his ministers ever gave the matter more than a moment's thought, if that. It's debatable whether the Fuehrer could even have pointed out the Severn on a map. (And he liked maps a lot.)

PRO-CATHEDRAL

By the 1830s Bristol's growing Roman Catholic population had outgrown its chapel in Trenchard Street, and plans were made for a huge new church. A plot of land was bought in Clifton, and Henry Goodridge (c.1800-1863), who had also designed Lansdown Tower and parts of Prior Park College in Bath, came up with plans for a large Classical-style building. The foundation stone for the Church of the Holy Apostles was laid in October 1834, but the project was dogged by problems. It was next to an old quarry and there were two, or possibly three, landslips.

Work was abandoned and the unfinished building – walls and six huge portico columns at only a quarter of their intended height – was put up for auction in 1844. In 1847 the Church bought the site back and a new, lightweight timber structure was constructed over Goodridge's building. This was designed by Charles Hansom (1815-1888), who would go on to become one of Bristol's leading Victorian architects.

In the 1870s, Hansom extended the building eastwards, but once more ambition ran ahead of reality and his plan for a spectacular 200ft-tall campanile was never realised. In 1850, Pope Pius IX formally reinstated Catholic bishops in England, and Holy Apostles was deemed a 'pro-cathedral', a church serving the temporary function of a cathedral until a permanent building was erected. It would not be until 1973 that Clifton Cathedral in Pembroke Road was opened. For many years after this, the Pro-Cathedral served as the Bristol Waldorf School.

The first proposal dates back to the 1840s, when engineer Thomas Fulljames drew up plans for a mile-long dam from Aust to Beachley. This would be a rail bridge and it would create a massive harbour which would take the ever-larger ships which were now being constructed. Fulljames was County Surveyor of Gloucestershire, and a significant part of his vision was that the barrage would be a huge boost for the port of Gloucester.

One reason why barrage plans have such a long history is because it would also be a bridge which would cut a significant chunk off the journey-time from England to South Wales. The structure which Fulljames put forward probably made good business sense, but the money simply wasn't available.

For the rest of the nineteenth century, talk of a barrage or dam across the Severn or Bristol Channel was intermittent. Talk of a bridge was very frequent indeed, though it was temporarily forgotten after the Severn railway tunnel was opened in 1886.

The first revival of the barrage idea came in 1901 when the directors of the Gloucester Dock Company looked once more into the possibility of creating a lake to make Gloucester into a major port. A barrage would enable it to handle the world's largest cargo vessels, and even the biggest battleships of the Royal Navy. Nothing came of this.

The Severn Barrage returned to the agenda seriously only at the end of the First World War. It has never been completely off the agenda since.

The proposal came from the Great Western Rail Company, which wanted a rail and road traffic bridge to relieve the pressure on the Severn Tunnel. GWR estimated the cost at between £6m and £8m. The idea was said to have come from a Mr J.F. Pannell, who worked in the company's chief engineer's office at Paddington as a result of a staff suggestions box scheme.

A Victorian company would have sought to raise the capital from banks and/or shareholders, but the First World War had changed everything. Now everyone knew that the government was a big spender on big projects. GWR approached the newly-formed Ministry of Transport, headed by Lloyd George's friend Sir Eric Geddes.

Geddes loved the idea. In 1920 his Ministry issued an outline proposal. This now-forgotten episode is significant, because electricity generation was mentioned for the first time.

The barrage would be a bridge, and it would be the largest hydro-electric scheme in the world, generating at a cost of just over half a penny per unit. It would save three to four million tons of coal per annum, and would create an immense locked basin on the upper Severn which could take the biggest ships.

To get over the issue of variations in tidal flow at different times of day, some of the power at peak times would be used to pump sea-water up to a reservoir high up the Wye Valley. At slack times this would be allowed to flow back down to drive the turbines to generate power. A breathless paper from the Ministry said:

The attractions of the scheme would appear to be limitless. They open up a vista which is little short of a revolution in the industrial life of the West and Midlands of England. It effectively solves the problem of congestion for all traffic

▲ Thomas Fulljames, *Proposed Barrage across the River Severn*. (Newport Museum and Art Gallery, South Wales/The Bridgeman Art Library)

between South Wales and the West of England both by road and rail, and brings within reach of all classes of the community the blessings of light, purity and power.

Geddes' own background was as a businessman, and the language is more akin to a share prospectus or an advertisement than a statement made by civil servants.

Significantly, there was no enthusiasm on the Welsh side of the river, where a saving of three or four million tons of coal a year was not something to be welcomed at all.

Fortunately for the Welsh coalfields, and the Exchequer, more sober heads pointed out that the scheme would have to be costed properly and a full technical feasibility study carried out. It was kicked into the long grass in 1921 when the government undertook a massive round of spending cuts, presided over by a committee on national expenditure chaired, coincidentally, by Sir Eric Geddes.

It was back again by 1924 when the government came under pressure from backbench MPs and the

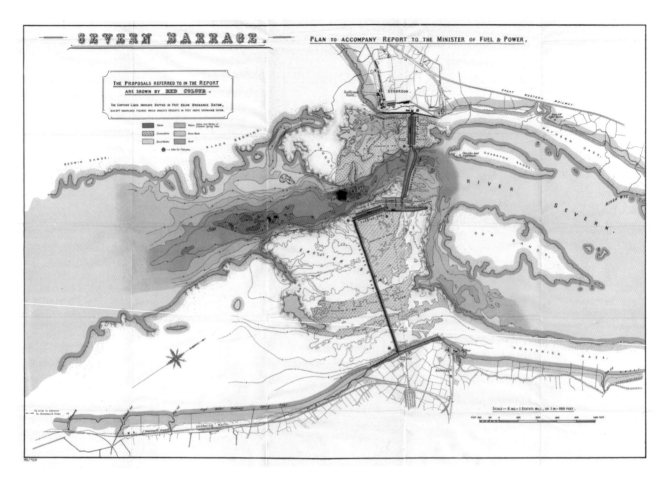

▲ From the Report of the Ministry of Fuel & Power on the Severn Barrage Scheme 1945. (Bristol Record Office Ref No: BRO 40997/1)

public. At a time of high unemployment, there were plenty of work-creation schemes around the country, and the barrage – which the original Geddes outline said would keep 10,000 men in work for seven years – would be one of the biggest ever. The government authorised a £95,000 study.

The resulting report was not published until March 1933 by the Severn Barrage Committee of the Economic Advisory Council. A barrage built in the recommended location at English Stones (the site of the present-day Second Severn Crossing), it said, would provide around 7% of the nation's projected electricity needs in 1941. It would take 15 years to complete over which time it would employ an average 12,000 men.

Bristol East MP Tony Benn looking at a plan for a Severn Barrage, 1971. (*Bristol Post*) ▶

When finished, it would be producing electricity at two thirds the cost of coal-fired power stations.

A third of the projected £38m bill was for the secondary storage plant, which would generate at low tide from water pumped up to the Wye Valley reservoir. This was despite that fact that in the meantime Paul Shishkoff, a Russian emigré, had invented a tidal generator which could spread the power output across 24 hours. Shishkoff had demonstrated his invention at Avonmouth in 1931.

Nothing happened for another ten years, partly because war got in the way. Then in 1943 a panel of experts appointed by the Ministry of Fuel & Power reviewing the 1933 report said that a barrage scheme was practical and could be economically justified. If work started in 1947, it could be finished by 1955, and be generating power before that. The cost would be £47m, but because of the huge expansion in supply and demand for electricity and the national grid, a barrage would be used with existing coal-fired stations, and so there would be no need for the secondary storage system.

And so it went on. The government occasionally commissioned studies, as did the nationalised electricity industry, the costs kept going up and the conclusion was always that it was more expensive than coal and/or oil, or that it was cheaper than fossil fuels, but the capital outlay was unaffordable for the time being. In the meantime, there were also alternative plans, such as that put forward in 1967 to impound water in two vast lagoons in order to generate a consistent power flow throughout the day.

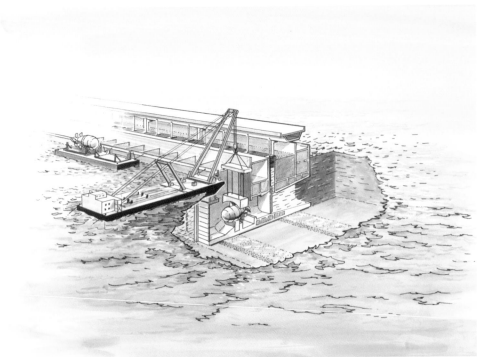

◀

Cutaway drawing from Severn Tidal Power Group showing construction of the caissons and installation of turbines

A major oil price rise in 1973 caused by the OPEC embargo set a pattern which would be repeated over the coming years. A crisis in energy costs and/or supply led to renewed calls for a barrage, but by 1975 the Central Electricity Generating Board was telling a Commons committee that Severn tidal power 'offers no prospect of producing electricity more cheaply than other means'.

In 1978 the Commons select committee on science and technology said an advisory committee on the Severn barrage should be set up urgently. Labour's Secretary of State for Energy Tony Benn (also Bristol East's MP at this time) appointed Sir Herman Bondi to head it.

The Bondi Comittee, reporting to the new Conservative government in July 1981 said that the barrage was technically and economically viable. It looked at several possible locations but plumped for Brean Down, just south of Weston-super-Mare, to Lavernock Point, between Barry and Cardiff. It would generate power using large pre-fabricated concrete caissons; the rising tide would flow through turbines (idling in reverse) and sluices, and generation would occur on the ebb flow as the water passed through the turbines. The whole thing would cost £5.6bn, but likely rises in coal and oil prices would justify the investment provided the government didn't opt to build more nuclear power stations instead.

In 1984 civil engineers Wimpey Atkins put forward a now-forgotten plan which represented a return to the Victorian solution. The Severn road bridge was too busy, and often forced to close in bad weather, and a new bridge was needed. Wimpey Atkins proposed a shorter, cheaper barrage between Severn Beach and Sudbrook Point in Gwent which would double up as a road crossing. This would be the eventual route of the M4 Second Severn Crossing. It would be a simpler and smaller barrage than that recommended by Bondi and could be built for £885m, which would be raised from the private sector. This plan failed because of worries over silting, and an alternative plan, known as the 'Shoots Barrage' was proposed a few years later by a former Atkins partner, Arthur Hooker working in conjunction with engineering firm Parsons Brinckerhoff. This was also close to the M4 Bridge route, and so shorter than the Brean Down-Lavernock route. It would cost less than £2bn and take four years to build. At the time of writing, this option is still in play insofar as some engineers and decision-makers think it the best option. A committee of Liberal Democrat MPs, Welsh Assembly members and councillors from Wales and South-West England endorsed the Shoots Barrage as their favoured option in 2009, a view adopted by the party nationally.

The most influential barrage vision in recent decades, however, is that of the Severn Tidal Power Group (STPG), a consortium of blue-chip engineering and construction firms (Balfour Beatty, Taylor Woodrow, Sir Robert McAlpine and Alstom). They carried out a huge study looking at all the different options and concluded that the 1981 Bondi report route from Brean Down to Lavernock was best. STPG also reckoned the power output could be larger, providing up to 6% of the UK's electricity needs. In 1989 the cost was estimated at £8bn. There would be 216 turbines: sluices would let the tide inwards, and then would be closed to force the water out through the turbines after the tide had gone out. There could, if desired, be a road and/or rail line running along it, though of course there would be locks to let ships through. The barrage debate would be dominated by the STPG plan for over two decades.

Already by the 1980s, conservation groups were voicing concerns about the likely effect on wildlife, while in more recent years the Bristol Port Company lobbied against a structure which could adversely affect its hugely successful business at Avonmouth, which is inside most of the proposed barriers. Many environmental campaigners endorse the idea of using the Severn to generate power, but say that options other than a barrage should be explored. For example, artificial lagoons could be created which would generate from the movement of water entering and/or leaving. The idea of a tidal 'reef' was endorsed in 2000 by the Royal Society for the Protection of Birds; this would be further downstream (and therefore longer) but with only a difference of two metres in level to either side. As it would not hold back the full force of the tide it was hoped that this would be less disruptive to ecosystems upstream.

Not unexpectedly, the Thatcher government baulked at the cost of the STPG plan, but the idea has been revived in public debate with more frequency and urgency ever since. With worries about global warming, rising fuel prices, and insecurity of supply, the idea has a lot of supporters. Whatever the fears for the wildlife, the barrage is usually presented in green terms. The STPG claimed its barrage would provide the same amount of electricity as three nuclear reactors and last for 120 years – and a lot longer if properly maintained. Once you get past the stupendous carbon-spend involved in building the thing in the first place – a workforce of 35,000 dropping immense lumps of concrete onto the sea bed – it's clean, green, sustainable, and produces no waste. Moreover, if we are to have rising sea levels and more extreme weather events, a barrage can play a significant role in flood protection.

In 2007 the Sustainable Development Commission, an independent advisory body to the government, produced a report saying that generating tidal power from the Severn (not necessarily using a barrage) was a sustainable option, and the government should look into it. The government did look into it, and in 2010 the Department for Energy and Climate Change's Severn Tidal Power Feasibility Study concluded that there was not, as yet, a strong enough case for building a barrage or other tidal power system. It recommended, however, that everyone keep an eye on the situation, and look out for opportunities from emerging technologies.

At the time of writing, several individuals and organisations are pushing for some sort of tidal system. Expect the debate to heat up again whenever there's some sort of climate or energy supply crisis. There'll be another one along at any minute.

Dockisation of the Avon
19th century – present

Nowadays the Floating Harbour is almost entirely a leisure facility, and the picturesque backdrop to offices, restaurants, bars and homes which have been built around it in recent decades. The port, however, used to be the city's entire reason for existing, the absolute hub of its economy.

To get a ship in or out of Bristol, you need to move it along the river Avon. In the Middle Ages, this was an advantage; the harbour was a safe haven which hostile shipping (including, in the seventeenth century, pirates from North Africa) could not easily reach.

By the nineteenth century, however, the trip along the Avon had become a major disadvantage. The Avon has strong currents, shifting mudbanks and is tidal. Specialist pilots with a lifetime of local knowledge were always needed to bring ships safely in and out of port. As marine engineering improved, ships grew ever larger, and so did the danger that they would become grounded on the journey up or down the river. The most hazardous passage was around the Horseshoe Bend near Pill.

The biggest ships of all had to wait for especially high tides to be sure of getting in or out of Bristol unscathed. When Brunel's ss *Great Britain* was launched in 1843 she was the largest vessel in the world. She left Bristol the following year, and never returned to Bristol again under her own power.

In 1851, the ss *Demerara*, the second largest ship built in Bristol up to that date, grounded and broke her back on the Avon on her maiden voyage. A

A terrible advertisement for the port of Bristol. The *Demerara* run aground on the banks of the Avon on her maiden voyage, 1851. (Bristol Record Office Ref No: BRO 43207/34/1/44) ▶

replica of her figurehead is in the city centre on the wall of the building next to the Hippodrome. There were other, similar disasters in 1874 and 1878, although the wreck which probably retains the best grip on local folk memory didn't occur until 1924 when the ss *Etrick* ran aground and capsized. Everyone in Pill, the story goes, got a new pair of boots that year. They were also well set-up for tobacco and chocolate, as they scavenged the hapless steamer's cargo, which had been jettisoned in an attempt to lighten her.

Ships running aground on the Avon were disastrous for the port's business. Not only was trade disrupted, often for several weeks, when a ship ran aground, but it was also the worst possible publicity for the harbour. The history of Victorian Bristol is littered with public debate about what ought to be done.

Various plans to make the river deeper were discussed. In 1859, for instance, the eminent engineer William Parkes recommended digging a new channel to by-pass Horseshoe bend.

The obvious solution was to build a port on the Bristol Channel coast, which, of course, is exactly what happened. Avonmouth dock opened in 1877, and another private company built a dock at Portishead in the 1860s which succeeded in taking a lot of the city's business. Both were quickly acquired by Bristol's Corporation.

Victorian Bristol, however, was also mesmerised by a different and more radical solution – 'dockisation'. The idea was to extend the Floating Harbour as far as Avonmouth, turning the whole tidal Avon from the centre of Bristol all the way to the Channel coast into one immense floating harbour. There would be

▲ Artist's impression from Business West's Bristol 2050 document 'High in Hope'. View of the hypothetical Avon 'linear water park' looking towards a remodelled Cumberland Basin. (Alec French Architects/Business West)

a dam at, or close to, the coast, and a system of locks for ships to enter and leave.

This was a bold and visionary idea, just the sort of thing you'd expect Victorian engineers to come up with. A succession of proposals was being seriously considered by the Corporation from the 1850s onwards.

The problem was the cost. Dockising the Avon was a major technical challenge, requiring far more than just a dam and some locks. There were all sorts of issues in preventing the new dock from silting up, and in ensuring that the city would still be drained properly. Not least was the question of Bristol's sewage, which was simply flushed, untreated, into the river at several points between Netham and Avonmouth. A tidal river carried (most of) this sewage away, but an enclosed dock would not; a massive new sewer system would be needed.

Again and again the city fathers discussed it, commissioning plans and engineers' reports and costings, and again and again they blanched at the price.

There were other concerns. In the Bristol Channel, near the mouth of the Avon is a stretch of water known to generations of seafarers as Kingroad. One engineer's report suggested that the outward flow of the river scouring the sea-bed kept Kingroad from silting up. Damming the Avon might well make the Channel impassable to large ships, so that they would not be able to get into the new dockised river anyway.

The last occasion on which the Corporation seriously considered the issue was in June of 1900. A report by some eminent engineers said that dockisation was a practical option; it would cost £2,775,000, plus around £500,000 for sewerage works, plus £250,000 for a passenger pier. It would also cost £36,625 a year to dredge the new harbour. At this time a skilled working man earned perhaps £80 to £100 a year. There are all sorts of ways you can try and translate the sums into modern values, but however you do it, the cost comes out as astronomical.

The plan was dropped, and Bristol's Corporation opted to build a new, larger dock at Avonmouth – the Royal Edward Dock, which opened in 1908.

Dockisation was barely mentioned again until the 1970s when the idea of a barrage at Avonmouth, Pill or Horseshoe Bend was briefly discussed as part of the wider debate about what to do with the City Docks when they closed as a commercial port.

It has now come back onto the agenda.

Late in 2011, local business organisation Business West published its Bristol 2050 vision, a set of ideas for how the city might look in 40 years' time. It was not intended as a blueprint for the future, but rather as a document to start local debate. It included several visionary suggestions, including a comprehensive network of footpaths and cycle paths, dramatically improved public transport, a massive remodelling of the Cumberland Basin area and an Avon Barrage close to the M5 bridge at Avonmouth. This barrage would generate electricity, and might well also carry a road or rail link, as well as turning the tidal river into a giant lake which could be used for boating, fishing and other leisure activities.

This is Victorian dockisation all over again, and in the coming years it will be discussed and debated every bit as earnestly as it was in the nineteenth century.

Within the next 30 years, there may well have to be some sort of barrier across the Avon. If sea levels rise and there are more extreme weather conditions, it will be needed to protect Bristol from floods. This might be a permanent structure, or it might be a moveable one, like the Thames Barrier. The cost will be considerable, and there will be huge concerns about the Avon's wildlife (which was not something that bothered the Victorians for a moment), but if Bristol were to experience regular large-scale flooding, the cost of not building it might be even greater.

Bristol Central Railway Station 1861-1863

Nowadays, the very suggestion of building a railway station in Queen Square would seem preposterous. Victorian Bristol, however, saw things differently. There had already been a proposal to run a line through the Square in the 1840s, but in the early 1860s a new rail company proposed building the city's principal rail terminus there. In those days there was no great civic, sentimental or aesthetic attachment to Queen Square. It was old-fashioned and carried with it unpleasant memories as the focal point of the notorious 1831 riot.

Brunel's Great Western Railway Station at Temple Meads was in an inconvenient location. Furthermore, the journey from Temple Meads to the city centre was not a pleasant one; the area between Bristol Bridge and the station was a warren of narrow streets, including some notoriously crime-ridden slums. The building of the wide new Victoria Street connecting the bridge to the station in the 1860s was as much a work of social as civil engineering.

The early 1860s saw a number of rail proposals all aimed at improving rail provision within the city itself.

It was the Bristol and Clifton Railway Company which proposed a station for Queen Square. The company prospectus was issued at the end of 1861 to general approval within the city. The firm was going to build a line from Temple Meads east to west through the city, through Redcliffe, across the water at Welsh Back, across Queen Square on arches and a low embankment. This embankment would also have accommodated a new main passenger station for the city, in Queen Square. The railway would then continue out along the line of Anchor Road to terminate at another station at the bottom of Brandon Hill.

The plan caused great enthusiasm and excitement locally, not only as it would bring passengers into the city centre, but also because it would serve the harbour. The line would be a direct link to the docks, with a new network of horse-drawn tramways on the Floating Harbour quays so that goods could be moved quickly from ships to trains.

It seemed a perfectly sensible plan. It was backed by many of the city's business leaders, including the Chamber of Commerce and the Society of Merchant Venturers. Most important of all, the Great Western Railway was on-side. The company would provide half the estimated £250,000 cost, borrow the rest at 4% and it would be the majority shareholder. What could go wrong?

Vested interests, in short. The arrival of a rail system right in the docks was a threat to the profits of some, and the livelihoods of many more – merchants, shipmasters, traders, warehouse owners, dock workers and lightermen. It would, said some, 'divert the commerce of the city'.

When, in March 1862, the Corporation met to consider the bill it would put forward to Parliament to approve the railway, it was presented with a petition against the scheme with 1,970 signatures on it. There were two other petitions as well, one from property owners on Queen Square who were naturally dismayed. Then, in a public relations stroke much remarked on at the time, Alderman Robinson (a ship-owner and former West India merchant), produced a further petition, this time signed by 150 Bristol washerwomen who feared a station on Brandon Hill would deprive them of their livelihoods.

At no point did anyone object on conservation grounds. The Queen Square residents were simply worried about the effect of the railway on the value of their properties. Nor does anyone seem to have been concerned about the effect that passing steam locomotives might have had, for instance, on the fabric of St Mary Redcliffe church.

The opposition continued when the Bill went to Parliament, where three Brandon Hill washerwomen appeared as witnesses. It failed at the committee stage.

An alternative scheme quickly followed. The Bristol Central Railway Station proposed a line from Temple Meads via Old Market to what we now call the Centre. The station here would have been roughly where the war memorial is today. This project did not have the backing of the Great Western, which by now had determined on improving Temple Meads (most of today's station was built in the 1870s). The scheme failed, apparently for lack of support. Another plan was put forward in 1863; the station would still be at the Centre, but this line would carry on southwards and join the Bristol & Exeter line in Bedminster. This would have required a tunnel running under the Floating Harbour and the New Cut.

This was a bold but viable scheme in the sense that Bristol city centre would have had a proper 'through' station connecting to all the other lines running through or near the town. It failed because Great Western and the Bristol & Exeter firms realised it would make Temple Meads redundant. There were also doubts about tunnelling under the docks.

Railway Mania (2) mid-1860s

The Bristol and South Wales Union Railway had knocked an impressive 93 miles off the journey from Bristol to South Wales. Passengers agreed it was a great improvement, but many Bristol businessmen were not convinced.

At this time, South Wales was undergoing one of the greatest booms of Britain's industrial revolution thanks to coal and iron. These were not materials which could be conveniently transported by the Bristol and South Wales Union route because goods had to be removed from trains, put onto the ferry, unloaded again and then put onto the train on the other side.

In the mid-1860s, two schemes were put forward. One was a proposal from a Great Western Railway engineer to build a new line from Wootton Basset in Wiltshire to the Old Passage on the Severn, plus an immense two-mile bridge over the river. This idea caused consternation in Bristol as it would take business from the city. In January 1865 some leading Bristol traders approved a visionary plan put forward by Charles Richardson, a friend of the late Mr Brunel and resident engineer on the Bristol and South Wales Union railway.

Richardson proposed a railway tunnel under the Severn costing £750,000 – a huge sum, but still less than half the cost of the bridge. Several leading Bristol businessmen gave the tunnel plan their enthusiastic moral support, although financial support was seriously wanting. As John Latimer, in his *Annals of Bristol in the Nineteenth Century* put it:

The construction of a tunnel four miles in length under an arm of the sea was not an enterprise likely to commend itself to any but robust-hearted investors.

Both the tunnel and bridge schemes collapsed following a banking crisis in 1866. The tunnel would, of course, eventually be built following several setbacks. Our failure to appreciate the monumental scale of this achievement, largely the work of Thomas Walker, who worked under the great Sir John Hawkshaw, is probably because of its invisibility.

Bristol Assize Court 1865-1867

In the mid-1860s, Bristol's city fathers were divided by a bitter row over a much needed new assize court. The episode came close to outright corruption, something quite abnormal for Victorian Bristol, where gentlemen may have treated the lower orders like dirt, but were usually gentlemanly to one another.

It started with 'the battle of the sites', a big debate over where the court should be. Several locations were discussed, but came down to either Queen Square, or an area to the rear of the Guildhall, fronting Small Street. The Guildhall site was small, and took in the remains of a twelfth-century hall house known as Colston's House, though it had no real connection with Edward Colston.

The Corporation hedged its bets by inviting designs for a court here, but also for a larger building in Queen Square. All but one member of the Bristol Society of Architects wrote a letter of protest, requesting a clearer brief. Only one proposal was submitted, by Pope and Bindon, the only firm which had not signed the letter. Richard Shackleton Pope (DoB unknown-1884) was at this time one of the city surveyors.

The Corporation's finance committee then announced a competition – prize 100 guineas (£105) – for new assize courts to be built 'in connexion with the Guildhall and if possible without interference with Colston's House'. Some 13 entries were received, and the winner was a design from Godwin & Crisp, the only one which had followed the brief faithfully.

Edward William Godwin (1833-1886) is thought by many to have been the greatest architect Bristol ever produced. His private life was also rather colourful. His court design was one of his characteristic forays into medievalism and would not only have preserved Colston's House but would have used it as a public hall. It opened to Small Street behind three arches with the same proportions as the ancient ones inside.

The judge's decision triggered a great deal of back-stairs intrigue by other local architects and a new competition was now announced. By now the row had gone national, with Bristol getting an angry memo from the Royal Institution of British Architects and signed by many leading architects of the day saying that a new contest would be a great injustice to the winners.

Nonetheless, the new contest went ahead and was won by Pope & Bindon in 1867, whose design is the one you can see in Small Street to this day. It is widely thought that Pope used his position in the council to swing the decision his way. Godwin appears to have thought so, referring to Pope as 'a wretched mean fellow'.

Such was the scandal that the RIBA set up a com-

: TEN HUNDRED AND SIXTY SIX :
A.D. 1871.

▲ Godwin's thwarted design for the Assize Court. (RIBA Library Drawings & Archives Collections)

mittee to examine future architectural contests around the country, and establish some ground-rules to ensure fairness.

Colston's House survived, incorporated into Pope's building but was destroyed by the City Architect's department in 1961.

Tidal energy from the Avon

1881-1883

In the early 1880s Bristol, in common with many other towns, was looking into the possibility of electric street lighting. In January 1881 seven of the newfangled electric lights were placed on the roads around the Council House in Corn Street.

The experiment was not a success. The generator used to power the lamps didn't work properly, and in any event electric lighting appeared to be more expensive than gas. Bristol's streets would be stuck with the smelly old-fashioned gas lamps for nearly two decades yet.

Local businessman William Smith, who also represented Clifton on the Council, thought he had a solution – why not use the tidal power of the Avon to generate electricity?

At a Council meeting in October 1881 he moved that the Sanitary Committee 'should be instructed to report to the Council as to utilising the energy to be obtained from the flow and reflow of the River Avon for the purposes of illumination.' By converting the tidal energy into electricity and storing it in Faure batteries, the city could save £6,000 or £7,000 per annum.

Smith's motion was voted down, but, undeterred, he travelled to the Paris International Electrical Exhibition just a few days later. There he met with Sir Charles Bright, one of the country's leading experts on electricity. Back in Bristol, Smith sent the local press a letter from Sir Charles saying that using the Avon to generate power sounded feasible. Furthermore, Sir Charles offered to travel to Bristol and carry out a preliminary study at his own expense.

He was as good as his word, arriving the following month. The visiting scientific dignitary was invited to hand out the prizes to the Trade & Mining School's best pupils in a ceremony at the Merchant Venturers Hall. Here he told reporters that it was completely practicable to power the city's lights using the Avon. There would, however, be costs and technical issues, he said. 'It is simply a question of comparative expenditure between that form of power and another.'

Meanwhile, Smith published calculations produced by Professor Sylvanus Thompson of University College Bristol showing the amount of energy produced by each tide at Totterdown (279,389 horsepower), Rownham (859,658 hp) and Avonmouth (2.1 million hp). Any one of these could produce more than enough power to run the city's existing 4,274 street lamps by electricity. Engineers wrote in to the local papers opining on the best place to site a tidal generation system, and speculated on what form it should take.

It would probably have been a barrage with a system of old-fashioned water wheels driven by the rise and fall of the tide, or it may have used a newer system of turbines instead.

By January 1882 Smith had persuaded the Council to set up a 'tidal force' committee to inquire into the issue and voted a small sum of money to have expert investigations carried out. Nothing seems to have come of it. By 1883 it was said that a report had been prepared by the eminent engineer Sir Frederick Bramwell.

By that summer, however, the local press was archly inquiring as to the whereabouts of Sir Frederick's report. Somewhere around this point the whole thing seems to have been quietly forgotten.

There are several likely reasons for the plan's demise. The first is that at this time Bristol was preoccupied with the possibility of dockising the entire tidal Avon. If this were to happen there would be no more tides to move the wheels or turbines.

There were also the engineering challenges. Sir Charles Bright had already pointed out that using the power of the tide was more complicated than simply harnessing a fast-moving river or waterfall. This would be a heavy task, requiring an array of large wheels (or, he suggested, floats) as well as a system of huge batteries to store electricity during those times when the tides were not producing enough motion. The effects of storms and ice on the river might interrupt the power supply and, more importantly, add to the maintenance bill for the system.

Challenging the Great Western (1) 1882-83

By the later nineteenth century, many in Bristol resented the monopoly position held by the Great Western Railway for passenger and freight travel between Bristol and London.

Thanks to the plethora of privately-owned rail companies criss-crossing the country, many other cities had more than one rail route to London, and many business leaders now felt that Bristol should enjoy a similar advantage.

The Bristol and London and South Western Junction Railway was formed to challenge the GWR. The company would need £1.86m in capital, but it enjoyed wide support across the city. The Corporation was behind it, the Merchant Venturers helped out with the expenses of getting it under way, and several of the city's most important businessmen backed the bill which was introduced in Parliament in November 1882.

Passengers would be able to travel to Waterloo Station, and could also access several places in the South and South-East England more easily. The line would leave the London & South Western line at Grateley, near Andover, pass through Westbury and go straight to Radstock where it would join the Bristol & North Somerset Railway, and go from there into the heart of Bristol via St Philips Marsh.

Had it been built, the impact on Bristol would have been huge. The line would cross over the Great Western Railway line in St Philips, then into Old Market, crossing Old Market Street on an ornamental bridge. From here it would go straight into the city centre and a passenger station situated where the Cenotaph is nowadays. There would be a large goods station at Lewins Mead.

There were public meetings in support of the scheme across the city, and as one observer noted: 'The whole city, indeed, seemed to be at one over the matter, and the unanimity was wonderful, both for its rarity and its vigour.'

The first setback was the likely cost of the new city centre station; that part of the project was postponed. Then, to cut a long story short, the plan failed in Parliament in the face of furious lobbying by the Great Western Railway, and by the opposition of Sir

John Lubbock, the member for London University, who was also a prominent scientist. Lubbock was dismayed that part of the line would run very close to Stonehenge, and indeed would cut straight across the Avenue and the Cursus. According to one report, one of the Bill's supporters made an unbelievably crass riposte: The Avenue was just a bank and a ditch, and as for the Cursus (which at this time was thought to have been a prehistoric running-track) … 'It might once have served as an ancient British racecourse, but all he could say now was that it was quite out of repair and no use whatever.'

Despite a proposed alternative route, the Bill was rejected. In the meantime, the Great Western and South Western rail companies entered into a non-aggression pact whereby they would do nothing to harm one another's business interests for ten years.

And so Bristol's hopes of an alternative rail route to London were killed off. For the time being.

Tramways Terminus 1895

In the 1890s, the Bristol Tramways and Carriage Company was one of the most powerful firms in the city. It had been operating horse-drawn trams since the 1870s and under the leadership of the formidable George White (later Sir George), it would now be the first in the country to electrify its system.

The different routes all converged in what we nowadays call the Centre, which is simply a shortened form of what the area was known as back then – the Tramways Centre.

The tram system carried tens of millions of passengers a year, and electrification would make it even more efficient and profitable. It would further fuel the outward growth of Bristol, making it possible for people to travel lengthy distances to work or to shop.

Not unnaturally the company decided it would like a landmark building at the Tramways Centre, and with Council approval it launched, in 1895, a competition to design a terminus building, with waiting rooms, lavatories and offices. The contest was won by the local partnership of Crisp and Oatley.

Oatley was, of course, George (later Sir George) Oatley (1863-1950), who would go on to become one of the most influential figures in Bristol architecture, his best-known legacy being Bristol University's Wills Memorial Building. At this time, though, he was a junior partner to the much older Henry Crisp (?1826-1896), whom he admired greatly both as a mentor and friend.

Crisp and Oatley's design was a remarkable one. The site was small – the middle of it was approximately where the statue of Edmund Burke is nowadays – and they came up with a triangular building with rounded edges. While it has plenty of conventional features, the domes at each corner give it a rather exotic, almost Middle Eastern appearance, or perhaps it was a hint of the famous Bristol Byzantine style which was all the rage when Henry Crisp was a younger man.

Despite the energetic support of George White, a man accustomed to getting his way, the plan ran into immediate trouble. Some of the shareholders didn't like it, and there were soon letters in the press saying it wasn't needed. More serious opposition came from the Council, where the Sanitary Committee pointed

Crisp & Oatley's design for the Tramways Terminus building, 1895 ▶

out (rightly) that as a waiting room it was too small, and as a building on that particular site it was too tall. The Company retorted that it was the Sanitary Committee that had wanted a clock on top of it in the first place, thus adding to the height. Then they got to wrangling over who should pay the estimated £5,000 cost of the building.

With the project bogged down, and with many people now saying that what was needed was just a plain simple shelter to protect tram passengers from the rain, the Company batted the whole thing back to the Council. The following year the Sanitary Committee did indeed hold a contest (prize: fifty guineas) for a shelter design. And then the whole idea was quietly forgotten.

Of course if it had been built, it would probably be a listed building by now. You can just imagine how it would have added to the complications of all the arguments about the layout of 'the Centre' ever since.

The Bristol Hippodrome opened in 1912, but for a while before that it looked as though the site might have become a

OATLEY DEPARTMENT STORE

department store instead. In 1908, a company was formed to build a 'palatial store' on St Augustines Parade. The prospectus pointed out that this was the centre of Bristol's tram system, and around 30 million of the Tramways Company's 48 million annual passengers got on or off here. The firm hired the local company of Oatley and Lawrence to design the building – this was George Oatley again, by now in partnership with George Lawrence (1872-1938). Note how this drawing, produced for the prospectus by the architect and artist Arthur Cecil Fare, artfully inserts a tram into the scene to re-emphasise the numbers of potential customers that would pass by the shop. It looks like a sound business proposition, but for some reason the plan fell through, and the site was sold to the firm which would build the Hippodrome.

Superior buildings sometimes never see the light of day. The Bristol architectural firm of Crisp and Oatley twice lost out in competition to an inferior

THE WRONG CHOICE?

architect. And Bristol was denied two good buildings. William Venn Gough (1842-1918) was one of Bristol's busiest architects, and has left his mark all over the city in everything from pubs to churches. He's not much liked by architectural historians, though; Pevsner described his Port of Bristol Authority building in Queen Square as a calamity. If you compare this fussy building with the more restrained plan (top right) put forward by Crisp & Oatley in 1884 you can see why. The losing design would have been far more in keeping with its surroundings.

Incidentally, Venn Gough and Crisp & Oatley were also in competition to build Colston's Girls' School on Cheltenham Road. Again, Crisp & Oatley put forward a more dignified proposal, but lost. Gough's winning design, with its alternating stripes of buff terra cotta and brick, produced a building which has been variously compared to streaky bacon or something made of giant Liquorice Allsorts.

Challenging the Great Western (2) 1902-03

In 1902, construction work on the modern new Royal Edward Dock at Avonmouth was under way, and a number of leading businessmen, headed by Charles Wills (a clothing manufacturer, no relation to the tobacco dynasty) formed the Bristol, London, and Southern Counties Railway. The company was seeking £6m in capital.

Once again, this was to link Bristol to London (Waterloo) via an alternative route to the Great Western's. It would also link to the new dock. Once again, there would be a new central station in the heart of Bristol, this time next to the Colston Hall. Nobody seems to have been overly worried that its construction would have entailed demolishing Christmas Steps.

The station would be on two levels; the lower for goods and the upper one for passengers, and a branch line from Avonmouth would join the main line close to the station.

From Bristol the line would go to Bath, where another new station would be built. From here it would run under Claverton Down to Monkton Combe, along the Avon valley to Bradford-on-Avon and Trowbridge and on to Urchfont in Wiltshire. Here it would skirt the edges of the huge military complex which was already growing on Salisbury Plain, which was potentially good for contracts with the War Office. It would go on to join the lines of two other firms, and so on into London.

The careful business calculation here was that it would bring Bristol, and its new port, within easy reach of a huge part of the population of southern England. At a meeting in Bristol in 1902 Wills himself said there was no point in having a port that could receive large cargoes if there was no way of getting those cargoes out to millions of people.

A Parliamentary bill was drafted, and the first directors were named, including Wills, John Mardon (paper and packaging), Sir Herbert Ashman (Bristol's first Lord Mayor, and a leather merchant), Thomas Lennard (boot manufacturer), Edward Robinson (stationery and packaging), George Davies (confectionery) and several others. There were the usual public meetings and the Council itself would seek the powers to contribute £100,000 of the capital.

When the bill reached the Commons in May 1903, it ran into the predictable opposition of the Great Western Railway and the (less expected) resistance of the London & South Western Railway. Several days of argument basically revolved around whether or not the company would ever be able to raise the £6m it needed.

Despite the pledges of several individuals and the optimism of the company that the public, especially people in Bristol and Bath, would be eager subscribers, less than £500,000 in firm commitments was on the table, and the bill was rejected the following month.

This was the last really big rail scheme ever put forward for Bristol, and the last time a station in the city centre was seriously mooted. In retrospect, one of the most interesting things is that its principal champions were mostly manufacturers. These men represented new money, rather than the older Bristol

CLIFTON ARCADE

Joseph William King is an enigmatic figure about whom little is known. He crops up as the occasional footnote in local history books, almost invariably described as an eccentric, or 'self-styled' architect.

King was certainly a builder, and lived in Clifton's Oakfield Road for at least some of the mid-to-late nineteenth century. He's best known, if at all, for what's now called the Clifton Arcade in Boyce's Avenue. This originally opened as King's Clifton Bazaar and Winter Gardens in April 1879 but was a commercial failure. King had hoped to make good on his investment by letting out shop units. For over a century it was a furniture storage warehouse but is now a characterful little shopping arcade of the type that King envisaged. All it lacks is the gardens and extensive greenery, indoors and outdoors, of the original.

King was responsible for some other buildings (e.g. the Royal Arcade, Whiteladies Road and 13-15 Clifton Road) but his most ambitious project of all never came close to being realised.

In response to concerns over the heavy traffic in the city centre, various people put forward proposals in 1874. King suggested an immense viaduct which would have run from a new 'circus' road junction connecting Broad Street and Bridewell Street. It would then rise over John Street, Nelson Street and Lewins Mead all the way up to the junction of Colston Street, Maudlin Street and Perry Road.

This plan is often dismissed as eccentric and fanciful, but from contemporary accounts it's clear that the Council gave it serious consideration, along with a couple of similar schemes, all intended to ease the traffic flows from Clifton to the centre. Whatever King's credentials, his plan was dismissed as too expensive, and because Bristol's commercially-minded burghers didn't like the idea of a new road that couldn't have shops along it. (Photograph: Stephen Morris)

BRISTOL'S AWAKENING.

'Bristol's awakening', as seen by local satirical magazine *The Bristol Magpie* in 1903. The Great Western Railway cheers as Bristol wakes up to find the Bristol, London, and Southern Counties Railway bill has been rejected. (Bristol Reference Library)

fortunes tied to shipping and trade. While their plans required what by the standards of the time was an astronomical sum of money, these were serious, hard-headed businessmen whose plan had been properly thought through commercially.

Just over a decade later, the new docks at Avonmouth would play a major, though largely-unpublicised, role in the war effort in the greatest conflict in history, bringing in food, war materials and even hundreds of thousands of horses. A modern and rapid rail supply link directly from the state-of-the-art Royal Edward Dock to London, via the immense military complex on Salisbury Plain, would have had a significant impact on the logistics of the war effort.

War Memorial 1919-1932

Discussions about a memorial to honour the Bristolians who had died in the First World War started shortly after the conflict's end, but it took years of heated argument before the Cenotaph in the city centre was unveiled in 1932. Bristol was one of the last of Britain's major cities to have a civic memorial.

Shocking and disrespectful? Well yes. And until it was unveiled in front of a crowd of 50,000 people, there had been a huge row about where it should be. Most people wanted it on College Green which, if you think about it, is a more appropriate place. In an age when most Britons were Christians (or at least said they were on official forms), a location outside the Cathedral would have appeared more seemly. It was also a more tranquil space than the city centre, and it was equally capable of accommodating large numbers of soldiers and civilians on Remembrance Day.

Why it ended up on Colston Avenue is something of a mystery. It's been suggested that it was part of some wider, though hidden, conflict within the two principal factions – Liberal and Conservative – of the local establishment.

By 1919, virtually every parish in Britain was considering its own particular memorial, and all the various communities and churches of Bristol were no exception. By the mid-1920s monuments had been erected in several locations around Bristol and its suburbs, and most are still the focus of Remembrance Day ceremonies. Many cemeteries also featured memorials; there's a particularly good one at Arnos Vale – 'Soldiers' Corner', unveiled 1921 – for instance. Schools, clubs and other organisations commissioned their own memorials, so for instance the Memorial Ground in Filton Avenue (opened 1921) was dedicated to the memory of the 300 or so Bristol rugby enthusiasts who had been killed in the war.

Each community tended to have a discussion over the best form that a memorial should take. One school of thought held that you should simply have some sort of monument, while an opposing view held that the money raised should be used not just to remember the dead, but to help the living as well. This is why a number of war memorial hospitals were built around Britain at this time.

(There were occasionally other debates, too. In Westbury-on-Trym it was decided that the war memorial should take the form of a stone obelisk. The local vicar, the Reverend J. H. Williams, condemned this as a 'pagan' symbol and in an act of breathtaking religious bigotry refused to attend the unveiling ceremony in 1920.)

As early as 1919 there had been talk of a city-wide memorial to honour the men (and a handful of women) who had died in the conflict. The Corporation set up a committee, and nothing happened. Early on it was decided that funding wouldn't run to a hospital, or care home or other such large amenity. One of the first proposals, though, was for something utilitarian – a Gothic cloister which also incorporated a bus shelter.

Bristol's civic memorial returned to the agenda in 1925, at a time when most of the other major cities either had one, or were building one. After lobbying by the newly-formed British Legion, a new committee, chaired by the Lord Mayor, was set up to raise funds and find a site. Given that the money wasn't

Bristol's war memorial, on Colston Avenue. In the wrong place? (Photograph: Stephen Morris)

going to be available for a hospital or home, most people agreed there should be a dignified, restrained and simple monument, an obelisk or cenotaph, probably. Unlike so many war memorials from previous eras, it should not glorify war. (The 'utilitarian memorial' argument did return a few years later, with a strong Council vote in favour, but this ignored financial realities and was forgotten once more.)

The argument, which grew bitter, was rather about where it should be. Suggested locations included College Green, Old Market, the Horsefair, Colston Avenue, the Downs and a few other places, but it came down to College Green versus Colston Avenue.

The committee recommended College Green, saying that the statue of Queen Victoria could be moved to another location (Victoria Park, Bedminster, was one suggestion). Discussion and letters in the local press revealed Bristolians were split on this issue; one ballot of readers showed a small majority in favour of keeping the old girl where she was. The issue remained in abeyance for a few years until the British Legion, by now actively raising funds at major public events, particularly football matches, organised a petition, signed by several ex-servicemen, requesting that the Dean and Chapter of the Cathedral allow the memorial on College Green.

'The Dean and Chapter do not find themselves able to grant the request,' came the reply.

Now, two local newspapers, *The Evening Times* and the *Times & Mirror* stepped in with a joint appeal which raised £1,700, and they launched a design competition, the winner to be chosen by the Lord Mayor's committee.

By this time, an annual Armistice Day ceremony was being held in the Centre and, after a lot of backstairs politicking, it appears that everyone decided that they just wanted to finish the job. The winning design, by local firm Heathman and Blacker, was chosen, and the Cenotaph was unveiled on Colston Avenue.

It may be that the full details of what was going on behind the scenes lurks in an archive or attic somewhere. If you want a conspiracy theory – and it is just a conspiracy theory – try this ... Like every other city, Bristol had plenty of statuary. Indeed, one of the reasons advanced for refusing the College Green site was that it already had Queen Victoria and the nineteenth-century replica of the Bristol High Cross. The history of many statues in Bristol tends to follow a similar pattern; there's a public appeal, the public don't donate enough money, and therefore a wealthy individual steps in to make up the difference.

▲ One of the alternative designs for Bristol's war memorial. This one came third in the contest. (Bristol Reference Library)

The war memorial was different; it was paid for thanks to tiny sums donated mostly by working people, many of whom had served, or had lost loved ones. The late 1920s and early 30s was a period of high unemployment and in Bristol a lot of left-wing agitation was spearheaded by ex-servicemen who had not returned to 'homes fit for heroes' as promised. Many unemployed former soldiers had been active in street protests over dole payments and the hated 'means test'. It might be (and this is just a conspiracy theory, remember) that some among the great and good feared any sort of agitation from ex-soldiers and were determined not to have such a popular and populist monument on College Green, one of the most privileged sites in the city.

King George V Memorial

1936-1982

King George V had been a popular monarch in Bristol. For one thing he'd visited the city far more often than his father or his grandmother. (Queen Victoria had notched up one solitary official visit in her entire reign. It lasted a single afternoon.) When he died in January 1936, everyone remembered the brilliantly sunny day that the King and Queen had come to open the University's new Wills building.

It was quickly decided that Bristol should memorialise the late King, and by the time plans were published in May 1937, drawn up free of charge by local architects, £5,000 had already been raised.

There would be two separate memorials. The first would be a children's playground in the Barton Hill/St George area. Land adjoining Feeder Road was bought, and £6,300 was spent on landscaping, play apparatus and a memorial gateway. 'King George's Playing Field' was opened by Lord Mayor Sir Francis Cowlin in July 1938.

The other part of the plan was for a 60ft-tall stone 'pylon' topped by a 16-sided bronze lantern which would be lit at night. Conceptually it was meant to reflect the late King's strong connections with the navy and navigation, and would also be appropriate to Bristol's maritime heritage. There would be granite steps at the base, and it would feature both the royal arms and those of the city of Bristol.

The Council was already planning a major new road (the 'Western Road') from St Augustine's to Victoria Street. This included a new bridge across the floating

▲ Artist's impression of the proposed George V Memorial. (Bristol Record Office Ref No: BRO PicBox/7/Plaque/17b)

▲ The King George V Memorial that actually got built

harbour in the Centre, and the Bristol Society of Architects' blueprint proposed covering over more of the harbour between this new bridge and the old one at Narrow Quay. This would create a new area from Colston Avenue to the new quay head, with the cenotaph at one end, and the new King George V memorial at the other.

In between would be an avenue of trees, lawns, flower-beds and fountains, and the new bridge head over the Frome would commemorate the builders of the British empire. The entire scheme, independent of the Memorial, was estimated at £100,000, and was adopted by the Council in July 1937.

When war broke out in 1939, the Council decided to scale back or defer several major projects. The revised scheme for the Centre included work to cover over the Floating Harbour, but the planned memorial was postponed.

After the War, there were intermittent discussions about it, with various alternative suggestions including,

apparently, a sunken pool and fountains, or a 68ft metal obelisk.

By the late 1960s, the memorial fund to which Bristolians had donated 30 years previously had reached about £8,000. The money was administered by the City Council and was something of an embarrassment as it could not be spent on anything else. There was even dark talk of corruption, and that some or all of the money had disappeared into someone's pockets, but this was certainly not the case.

In the end, a memorial was built using the donated funds, though one imagines that scarcely one Bristolian in a hundred could point it out.

It is the arched fountain near Broad Quay House. On one side is the face of a lion, and on the other are two statues – a farm worker and coal miner – which were salvaged from the old Co-operative Wholesale Society building which had stood on the site of Broad Quay House until it was demolished in the 1970s.

The two figures were from a set of six representing different occupations which had stood over the CWS building entrance. Many Bristolians felt it would be a shame if they were lost and so two were incorporated into the memorial, which was paid for by the King George V memorial fund and unveiled by Lord Mayor George Maggs in May 1982. Whatever the fountain's artistic merits, it is the product of a bizarre compromise.

QEH KINGSWESTON

In 1935 Kings Weston House was bought by Bristol Municipal Charities, which intended to move Queen Elizabeth's Hospital School there from its location in Berkeley Place. The old kitchens were demolished and building work started on the school's new dormitories. Work was halted by the outbreak of war in 1939, and the work was never completed. The ruins are still there near the house to this day, while some of the masonry can be spotted lining footpaths nearby.

Replanning Bristol 1941-1948

Bristol was Britain's fifth most heavily bombed city during the Second World War. Between the earliest raids in 1940 and the last one in 1944 Bristol endured 77 German attacks in which over 900 tons of bombs were dropped.

Most of these were small attacks involving one or two aircraft. There were, however, six major night-time raids over the winter of 1940-41 which destroyed or severely damaged large areas and caused hundreds of deaths and many more injuries each time. In all, 1,299 people lost their lives in the Bristol Blitz.

The first major raid took place on the night of November 24/25 1940. In terms of Bristol's built environment, it was also the most destructive, and we live with its legacy to this day.

Until that night, Castle Street – which ran east to west through what is now Castle Park, along with Wine Street, running parallel with it to the north – was Bristol's principal shopping area. These two streets, and those around it, were a dense warren of fairly narrow streets and buildings, most of which had sprung up in the decades after Bristol Castle was dismantled in the 1650s.

Because most people in those days still worked on Saturdays, or Saturday mornings at least, the area came alive on Saturday evening with families out shopping, visiting the cinemas and cafés, or just promenading. Housewives, especially, liked to come on a Saturday evening knowing that butchers would have to sell off their stocks because they didn't have adequate refrigeration to keep meat until the following Monday.

On that fateful night, the heart of old Bristol was destroyed. As in subsequent raids, most of the damage was done not by high explosive bombs, but by incendiary bombs which started fires that overwhelmed the emergency services. You can still see this today in the burned out shells of St Peter's Church, or Temple Church, or St Mary-le-Port, with scorch marks occasionally still visible in the stonework.

The destruction of the Castle Street area also severely disrupted the city's flow. Until November 25 1940, there had been a more-or-less continuous shopping street running from Blackboy Hill in the north, down Whiteladies Road, down Park Street, through the Centre, on through Castle Street, into Old Market, West Street and on to Stapleton Road in one direction, or off to Kingswood and ultimately London in the other.

The first reconstruction plans were being mooted well before the war had even ended, and the issue understandably dominated local debate. In all this, one individual stands out above all the others.

John Nelson Meredith had been appointed Bristol's first City Architect in 1938. City planning was formally still the domain of the City Engineer's Department until the 1970s, but J. Nelson Meredith played a leading role in shaping the post-war city.

'Bristol should arise anew, noble and strong, beautiful and full of character, with no loss of its traditions and glories,' he told a meeting of the Bristol Kyrle Society (renamed the Bristol Civic Society in 1943) in November 1941. 'Surely it is well worth the struggle and the cost. We must build again – and build better.

'In all buildings we should insist on good, simple and dignified architecture. In the past there have been too many frills introduced. These should be cut out

▲ 'Bristol should arise anew, noble and strong, beautiful and full of character, with no loss of its traditions and glories.' City Architect J. Nelson Meredith.
(Bristol Record Office Ref No: BRO 40826/COU/6/1)

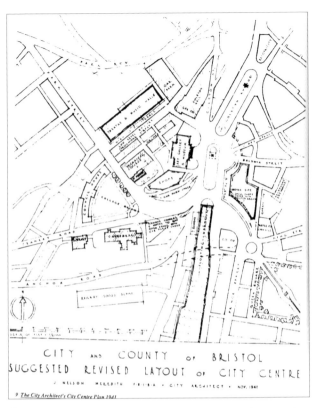

▲ Thinking aloud. J. Nelson Meredith's 'Revised Layout of City Centre' from 1941. Note the area set aside for culture and education next to the Council House (which was not yet complete)

entirely, so also should all shams, such as imitation half-timber.'

Meredith appealed for local materials to be used as far as possible, and looked forward to the creation of a city that was comfortable to live in, as well as 'orderly and pleasant to look at.'

In the case of Bristol, as in almost every other British city, 'planners', particularly those active between 1945 and 1975, are generally blamed for many urban ills. These faceless bureaucrats foisted dreary concrete vistas on us where once there had been ornate or characterful old buildings made by craftsmen. The planners drove massive, noisy roads through areas of priceless heritage, and tore down happy working-class communities where folk never locked their doors at night, and drove people into crime-ridden tower blocks instead.

The truth of this caricature can be argued over. It is

certainly the case that during the immediate post-war period, the officials and elected members of Bristol's Corporation displayed a haughty disdain for the feelings of ordinary Bristolians. In fact, they didn't take too much notice of civic or business groups either.

It is important, however, to see their plans in context. Men like J. Nelson Meredith, who had previously been City Architect in Norwich, had forged their early careers at a time when 'slum clearance' was one of the overriding priorities of local councils. In Britain's bigger town halls, the principal job of a City Architect at this time was the design and construction of housing.

To these people, old buildings were not necessarily beautiful or interesting; many old buildings were overcrowded, rat-infested, jerry-built and thoroughly deserving of the wrecking ball. Everyone had a right to decent housing and a decent work environment. The new homes would have gardens, and be built on bright, airy estates on the city's outskirts. It was also axiomatic that car ownership would increase with the return of peace and prosperity. One day, even the working man would be travelling to the factory in a car of his own.

For all its horrors, the Blitz offered the chance to build a brilliant new city where the mistakes of the past would not be repeated. Again and again in books and newspaper articles from the time, we encounter words like 'clean', 'hygienic' and 'healthy'.

The other term one encounters is 're-planning'. Not re-building. At no point did it occur to anyone in power in Bristol that they should simply re-build on bomb-damaged areas. This was simply not on the table. They wanted to re-order the city on a vast scale.

If realised, these plans would have demolished huge numbers of undamaged buildings as well.

The plans which were produced for Bristol, both by the Council and other organisations, may appear brutal to us, or unrealistic, in some cases downright insane. That's because these men (they were all men) were intoxicated by the clean slate that the Blitz appeared to offer them. They meant well.

The Council's earliest tentative plan from the spring of 1941 (before the last major raid had even taken place) set the tone for later ones, placing huge emphasis on traffic and transport. There would be an inner circuit road, car parks and a bus station. The main through roads would not be shopping streets. These plans in turn were based on pre-war ideas; the first car park, or 'parking garage' as it was called, had been proposed for Trenchard Street in the late 1930s.

Meredith's plan of November 1941, with its open spaces and wide roads, also envisaged a major 'cultural centre' for Bristol in the area between College Green and the Colston Hall. As well as the Colston Hall there would be a theatre and music hall, a museum and art gallery, shops and plenty of car parking, some of it underground.

This plan was only ever a set of suggestions, none of which could possibly have been implemented in wartime.

The Bristol Central Area Replanning Scheme was unveiled to the public at an exhibition at the City Museum in March 1944, and was far more serious. Everyone knew the War would soon be won (over by Christmas, some said), so now it was time to get down to the business of rebuilding.

The Scheme was the work of the departments of

the City Engineer and the City Architect, and had been endorsed by the Council's Planning & Reconstruction Committee. Many of its recommendations would eventually be implemented and have had a major impact on the city ever since.

Heavily damaged areas would be reconstructed, and there would be an inner ring road connecting to radial roads. The report also divided the city into separate zones for different activities – shopping, education, business, industry, warehousing and homes. A huge part of Kingsdown, for example, was designated a 'university and hospital centre'. Zoning also meant that central Bristol would cease to be a residential area for decades to come.

One of the key aspects of the plan was that Bristol should have a brand new shopping centre. The loss of the shops in and around Castle Street/Wine Street was going to be felt acutely when the city returned to a peacetime economy, and the plan proposed 32 acres of traffic-free retail development in Broadmead. Much of the impetus for this new shopping centre followed lobbying by the larger retail chains who wanted more space in which to build bigger shops and stores, and who had felt restricted by the cramped conditions in pre-war Wine Street/Castle Street.

As to the heavily bombed former shopping area, the report suggested: 'The area roughly bounded by High Street, Wine Street, Fairfax Street, Lower Castle Street, Castle Ditch, the Counterslip, Bath Street and Bristol Bridge shall be reserved as a public open space with a limited number of buildings upon it.' In other words, what is now Castle Park should be an open space. In the years to come, however, there would be other plans for this area.

The 1944 scheme also suggested that this open area might be a good location for a conference centre and an underground car park. It said that the remains of St Mary-le-Port and St Peter's churches, gutted by firebombs in November 1940, should be left in place. The remains of St Peter's Hospital, an elaborate seventeenth century half-timbered building which had served for much of its history as a workhouse, should also be preserved. The church remains are there to this day, but of St Peter's Hospital there is no trace.

The 1944 document generated plenty of opposition. Many small traders feared that moving northwards to Broadmead would be bad for business. Other people feared (rightly) that the link between the city centre and Old Market would be lost.

There were counter-proposals. Bristol Rotary Club came up with a dignified and visionary plan to turn the south side of the river between Bristol Bridge and Counterslip into a park. There would be a major civic centre on the site of Castle Park. Part of the ambition of this plan was to bring more green open space into the centre of the city.

The Western Counties Chapter of the Incorporated Association of Architects & Surveyors (nowadays the Association of Building Engineers) responded by filling in more detail of the proposals they had exhibited the previous year.

Their 'Plan for Bristol', also published as a brief pamphlet in 1944, is an astonishing work of 1940s futurism and idealism. Among other things it proposed a Severn Barrage, adding that the level and stable stretch of water created above the Barrage would then be an ideal 'regional base for commercial flying

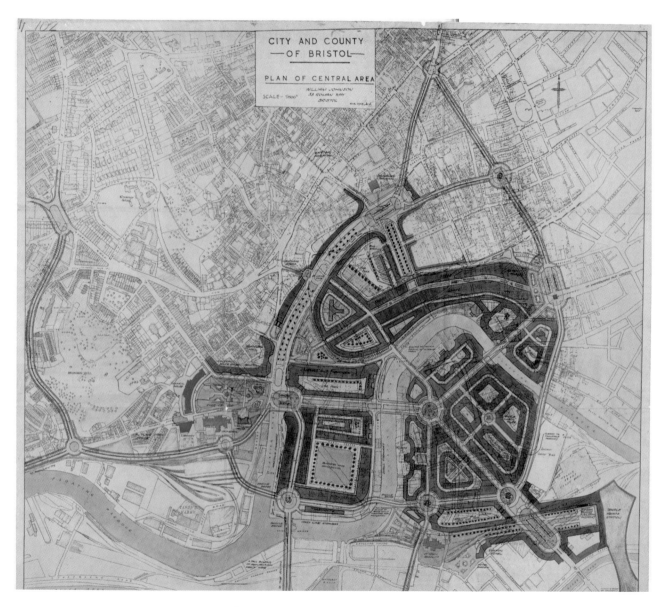

▲ Plan of central Bristol drawn up in 1943 by City Engineer William Johnson, showing
possible re-developments and zones for separate activities.
(Bristol Record Office Ref No: BRO41964/WJ/7)

Bristol Rotary Club's vision for post-war Bristol from 1944 included the new Broadmead shopping centre, and a civic/cultural centre at Castle Park. The George's brewery site across the Bristol Bridge would have been cleared to make way for a park

boats, one of the few which would be required for the country as a whole.'

The Plan for Bristol also envisaged turning a huge area of the Centre into a 'Central Park' with lawns and gardens and making a feature of the stretch of the Floating Harbour coming into the Centre. 'Within this area, at the foot of the slope on which the Cathedral stands, is planned a pleasure water formed from the existing waterway and flanked by terraces. From these motor-craft would be able to ply as of yore carrying passengers up and down the reaches of the river.'

Actually, to modern eyes the Plan for Bristol looks absolutely horrible.

A Central Park and flying boats are all very well, but the buildings were all to be brutal, monotonous blocks straight out of Stalinist Eastern Europe. Or as one study put it, the architecture 'seems to have been modelled on the 1930s Canons Marsh tobacco bonds.'

The Council approved its own plans in the summer of 1945, despite mounting concerns over the costs and scale, and submitted its proposals to Whitehall the following spring. These included a bid for the compulsory purchase of 771 acres of land, later slightly reduced, at an projected cost of £26m, a sum which was considered a major under-estimate.

At the subsequent inquiry held by the Ministry of Town and Country Planning, there were almost 300 objections. The barrister for the objectors contended that only 80 acres destroyed or damaged by bombing need be bought out. He added that it would involve

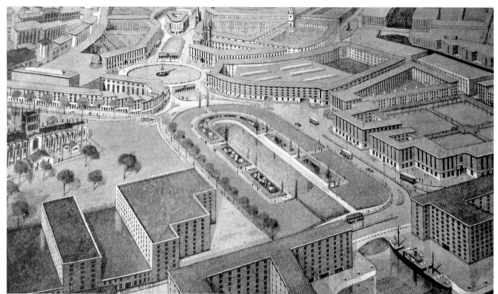

► Flying boats on the Severn, and Stalinist blocks around Bristol's Central Park. The Western Counties Chapter of the Incorporated Association of Architects & Surveyors' idea of the new Bristol

a great deal of unnecessary destruction of buildings, in some cases merely in order to make roads wider.

While the men from the Ministry went away and deliberated, the Bristol Retail Traders Association (RTA) came up with their own riposte to Broadmead. They wanted to put shops back in the Wine Street/Castle Street area, with a massive development of around 300 shops, including department stores, which could be approached on different levels.

This was another of the astonishingly radical designs produced in this period. The shopping complex would be bounded by a road suspended along the front of the buildings, like an enormous shelf.

The RTA proposed calling it New Upper Bridge Street and at the corner overlooking Bristol Bridge this road would have risen to a height of 75ft. Not only would it have permitted access to the new shops, but

it would have also acted as a through road for the city.

Pedestrians would reach the shops via ramps at Old Market and Bristol Bridge, which would have been covered to protect from rain. In the middle facing out over the water, would be gardens and a piazza around the ruins of St Peter's church.

The RTA claimed that while this scheme looked expensive, in fact it might be less costly than Broadmead. As a high-rise development it required less land, and less infrastructure than Broadmead, and as it would be built on rock it would need less foundation work. The Council's Planning & Reconstruction Committee politely accepted the plan, and proceeded with Broadmead anyway.

In December Bristol got its response from the Ministry. Most of the 771 acres the Council wanted, it said, did not fit the statutory definition of areas that

▲ The Bristol Retail Traders Association wanted Castle Street back, along with a major shopping complex with a road running around it, suspended like an enormous shelf. This was how it was envisaged, looking towards Castle Street from Old Market

had been 'war-damaged or contiguous thereto'. It proposed that the Council could have 245 acres in an area which did not include the Centre, Park Street or any of Clifton. The Ministry, like most of the objectors, thought the Council plan too ambitious.

Meanwhile, Clement Attlee's Labour government was desperately struggling against all manner of economic problems simply to meet the population's most basic needs. The Ministry cut Bristol's plans again the following year, and in any event the government – which would have been expected to cover most of the replanning costs – had no money available.

At a time of budgetary cuts and chronic shortages of building materials, the very idea of demolishing habitable buildings, no matter how shabby they were, made no practical sense. The idealism and optimism, and the visionary dreams of victory, were severely blunted by the cold, pragmatic realities of peacetime.

In April 1948, following even more budget cuts, the Ministry decreed that only land that was urgently and essentially needed could be purchased. Bristol's weary officials, councillors and aldermen (many of whom, by now, were considering resignation), returned with a plan to buy 19 acres for Broadmead. In September that year, the Ministry allowed Bristol to buy just four and a half acres in order to start work on the new shopping centre.

In 1945, the country had emerged victorious from

the greatest conflict in history and anything seemed possible. But just a few years into the peace, almost nothing seemed possible anymore. While nowadays we can give thanks that most of the planners' visions weren't realised, it's hard not to feel some sympathy for them, and for the councillors who battled Whitehall, who asked for 771 acres ... and came away with just four and a half.

Bomb-sites with buddleia bushes growing wild on them would remain a common sight well into the 1980s. The rebuilding of the city had to proceed in a piecemeal fashion, and there would be many more abandoned schemes along the way, though few would be as huge, as imaginative, or as idealistic as those which were produced in the 1940s.

Broadmead 1946-1960

Broadmead was the special project of City Architect J. Nelson Meredith. Unlike the rest of the Corporation's plans for post-war Bristol, which had been drawn up in collaboration with the City Engineer's Department, the new shopping centre was almost entirely Meredith's own work. It would also be his most visible legacy to Bristol.

Broadmead, at least until its cosmetic makeover of the early 2000s, would become a byword among Bristolians for a dreary, joyless retail experience. This, however, was not entirely Meredith's fault.

His original concept was for a number of blocks of four five-storey buildings arranged around a crossroads. Many old buildings had survived the Blitz and would be demolished, but some important heritage sites would be preserved. John Wesley's House and Quaker's Friars would become important features set in piazzas of their own. The old Greyhound Hotel would remain in place. Meredith, aided by vigorous campaigning by the Council for the Preservation of Historic Bristol (chaired by Sir George Oatley) also succeeded in persuading his masters to restore the Lower Arcade, which dates back to the 1820s.

Broadmead would be completely pedestrianised, and shoppers would be protected from the elements by covered ways and arcades, and a continuous canopy which would have run along the frontage of all the shops. With its low-rise buildings, open spaces, colonnades and extensive use of Bath Stone, the overall effect would have been a sort of restrained modernist Georgian style. A lot, in fact, like an updated version of Bath.

The plans were unveiled in 1946, but as with the wider replanning of the city, the Council was continuously frustrated by lack of funding and permissions for compulsory purchase.

Six years later, only nine shops had been built, and the development of the site would continue in fits and starts until more or less complete in 1960. Aside from the lack of money, the plan was also scuppered by the individual shops. Woolworths, for example, insisted on having its customary big red fascia at the front of the store, so the continuous canopy covering shoppers had to be broken. Other stores insisted on designing their own premises.

It would be 1977 before Broadmead would be pedestrianised, and then only partly. For decades one of the most depressing vistas was Quakers Friars, a medieval building which Meredith had wanted to

CITY & COUNTY OF BRISTOL — PLANNING & RECONSTRUCTION COMMITTEE
DESIGN FOR NEW SHOPPING PRECINCT
Perspective View from point B looking North-West
J. NELSON MEREDITH — F.R.I.B.A. — CITY ARCHITECT
P. R. STEELE — F.R.I.B.A.-F.I.-A.M.T.P.I. — CHIEF ASSISTANT ARCHITECT

make the focal feature of an open, relaxing piazza, but which actually ended up standing in the middle of a car park next to a public toilet.

▲ Broadmead, as envisaged by City Architect J Nelson Meredith (Bristol Record Office Ref No: BRO PicBox/7/Replan/4b)

The Council House Nudes

1945-1948

Building work on Bristol's new 'Municipal Building', as the Council House was called, started in the 1930s, but was put on hold for the duration of the Second World War.

The entire project was, not unexpectedly, dogged by all sorts of local controversies about aesthetics and how much ratepayers' money was being lavished on this palace of local government. The original cost in the mid-1930s had been estimated at £462,000, but by the time it was finished the bill added up to £1.3m. Some £10,000 of this was on account of the architect's insistence that the whole of College Green be lowered by several feet and flattened out to make the building look all the more imposing from the front.

There was also a major row about nudity.

Architect E. Vincent Harris had decided that there would be an ornamental 'moat' in front of the building. If you look at it today you might notice that the fountains at either end are curiously bare-looking. If you look closely you'll even see that the plumbing is showing. As though there was supposed to be something on top. That's because there was...

Harris wanted the fountains to be ornamented, and the celebrated sculptor Alfred F. Hardiman RA was engaged. Harris had also hired Hardiman to produce two bronze unicorns for the new building, and it is thought that these had actually been cast, but were lost when Hardiman's London studio was destroyed in the London Blitz. The unicorns on the Council House roof nowadays were made after the War by

▲ Hardiman's half-size model of the proposed bronze figure for Bristol's new Council House. The structural support between her legs is an owl – symbol of night – that has just pounced on a lizard – symbol of day. (Aberdeen Art Gallery)

David McFall.

Hardiman's plan for the fountains was for two bronze nudes entitled *Night* and *Day*. *Night* was going to be colossal – 30ft tall – and was presumably intended to be framed by the arch at the southern end of the building. *Night* was modelled on Nyx, the mysterious ancient Greek goddess of the night. *Day*, who would be rising out of the fountain at the Park Street side was, according to various reports, either going to be another goddess, or maybe Helios-Apollo, the sun god. This would presumably be of a similar size, although one press report from the time says *Day* was going to be male, and that he would only be one third the size of *Night*.

Hardiman made a half-scale maquette of *Night* which was exhibited at the Royal Academy in 1945 and won a silver medal from the Royal Society of British Sculptors the following year.

Harris approved the designs, but now the plan ran into fierce controversy. There were soon letters in the local press expressing dismay that a massive naked woman was going to be positioned right next to the Cathedral. 'A shameful flaunting of human nakedness in the face of God,' said one. 'A modern goddess of sex!' thundered another. Soon, the correspondence melded into wider complaints about the cost of the entire building, and the vandalism of Harris's landscaping of College Green. Naturally, *Night* had her defenders. One *gallant* suggested that if prudes didn't like the look of her, they should wear their gas-masks when walking past.

◀ An impression of what *Night* might have looked like in situ, created by Bristol art historian Anthony Beeson.

The Dean and Chapter of Bristol Cathedral came out against the statue as well, but Harris, and the Council, stood their ground. In the autumn of 1945 the Municipal Buildings Committee said that after very careful consideration it was satisfied with the artistic merit of the figures and the importance of them in the architect's plan, and that it would not give its backing to any changes.

And yet the statue was never made. The reasons for this are complicated and obscure, although we can presume that it might have been difficult to cast such an enormous bronze in the immediate post-war years because of material shortages.

Hardiman died in 1949 and his widow entered into a dispute with the Council over payment for the work he had done. The Council claimed it had never entered into any firm contract.

The 18ft maquette, meanwhile, appeared in the 1951 Festival of Britain's sculpture exhibition in Battersea Park and eventually ended up in Aberdeen Art Gallery, where it remained on display into the late 1950s or early 60s. It then went into a church (!) for storage, but alas, succumbed to vandalism and/or age.

The episode lived on in local folk memory for many years as a triumph of the petty philistinism for which Bristol used to be notorious. As early as 1950 the *Western Daily Press* said *Night* was 'jilted for her brazen symmetry which might have shocked the piety – or prudery – of the public.'

What shall we do about Castle Park? 1958-present

Fifteen years after the Blitz, the former Wine Street/Castle Street area was still vacant, and still earmarked – 'zoned' – for 'culture-amenity' purposes as laid out in the post-war reconstruction plans. In April 1958, the Council decided to lease some of the land on the site for two office buildings.

This led to a protest from the Bristol Architects Forum (BAF), a group of radical young architects and students founded in opposition to the (in their opinion) stuffy and conservative Bristol Society of Architects.

The BAF submitted a report and outline scheme to the Council for the redevelopment of the whole site. They proposed a new museum, a technical library and 'trade centre' intended to attract business and industrial conferences and trade fairs. The whole thing, as per the 1940s plans, would be set in a landscaped parkland.

The Council's Planning and Public Works Committee invited further proposals and had about a dozen from different organisations, including the Civic Society, the Bristol Society of Architects, the Round Table and even the Workers Educational Association. Meanwhile, a campaign supported by the *Evening Post* collected 11,500 signatures for a petition against the office development, leading one irritable councillor to suggest that opponents should stand for election to the Council. The Royal Fine Art Commission stepped in, too, suggesting that the office development should be dropped as the site offered an excellent opportunity for a comprehensive scheme at the historic heart of Bristol.

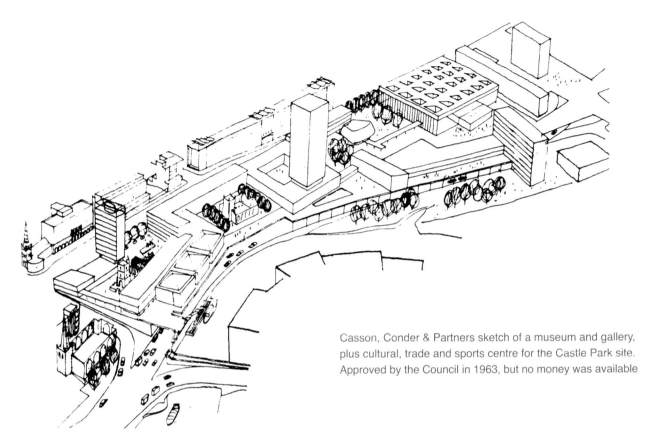

Casson, Conder & Partners sketch of a museum and gallery, plus cultural, trade and sports centre for the Castle Park site. Approved by the Council in 1963, but no money was available

The Council ignored all these, and even more acute concerns when the plans for the buildings were published. These would go on to become the Norwich Union and Bank of England buildings, close to Bristol Bridge. At the time of writing they are derelict eyesores, and all the most dire predictions about how ugly and inappropriate they would be have more than come to pass.

But public pressure had worked up to a point. The developments took up a relatively small part of the site, and in 1961 the Council started drawing up plans for a new £1.5m Cultural Centre, plus the promised parkland. Announcing the move, Planning Committee chairman Gervas Walker said: 'Wouldn't you rather have Castle Park than Castle Street?'

The Council later went on to commission the leading architectural firm of Casson, Conder & Partners to design a museum and gallery, plus cultural, trade and sports centre. The blitzed remains of St Peter's and St Mary-le-Port were to remain on the site. The resulting blueprint was approved by the Council in 1963.

And then nothing happened. The money simply wasn't available. By 1968 the estimates had doubled.

The Dutch House and below, the formerly bustling Castle Street derelict and undeveloped for decades before being turned into a park

THE DUTCH HOUSE

One of the losses that Bristolians felt most keenly after the Blitz was that of the Dutch House, which stood on the corner of High Street and Wine Street. It was built during Bristol's first great speculative building boom, when the Castle was demolished in the late 1600s, freeing up a huge amount of land for shops and housing.

The building, used at various times through its history as offices, a shop and homes, was a much-loved landmark at the centre of the old city, and featured extensively on postcards and railway posters.

It was badly damaged in the first major air raid on Bristol in November 1940, and was demolished a few days later by a company of the Royal Engineers who had been sent to the city to assist with clearing up and making damaged buildings safe.

It has been claimed that the Dutch House could have been saved, and ever since there have been periodic calls for it to be rebuilt on the same site. In 2012, for instance, Bristol Mayor and architect George Ferguson said that Bristol should rebuild some of the architectural treasures lost in the war. A new Dutch House, he said, could either be a faithful reconstruction, or it could just as well be a contemporary equivalent.

In 1969, the Arnolfini art gallery – located in Queen Square at this time – came forward with a proposal. They commissioned Casson, Conder & Partners, with Council approval, to draw up plans for an arts centre on the site. There would be a gallery and exhibition space, a 500-seat cinema, a 300-seat performance space for music, theatre and dance, craft workshops and a bar and restaurant. The latter would also offer fashionable 'cordon bleu' cookery courses for the aspiring middle classes.

Better still, the Arnolfini came with money – £200,000 from a wealthy anonymous donor, plus the confident expectation of funding from various bodies. This would go a long way towards meeting the anticipated £425,000 price tag of the development. In return, the Arnolfini wanted a low ground-rent for the site. The Council was being offered a solution to the Castle Street problem on a plate, and one which met both public expectations and its own designation of the site as a culture-amenity zone.

The Council, however, would still have had to spend money on the area, particularly the landscaping. For this, it was hoping that Bristol University would purchase the old City Museum on Queen's Road, but this deal fell through, either because the University couldn't raise the money, or because it decided it didn't want the building anyway. Meanwhile, the system for government funding of such projects changed. The plans were shelved, the Arnolfini moved to what is now the Watershed, and in 1975 took up residence at Bush House, where it's been ever since.

The Castle Street bomb site had, for some time now, been a large (and frankly pretty convenient) car park, though perhaps the lowest point in its history was reached in the early 1970s when it was suggested that it might be a good place to put local courts and administration buildings.

Finally, Casson, Conder were asked to simply draw up a plan for landscaping the site. This included a palm house, and would have exposed much more of the ruins of Bristol's medieval castle than are visible today. The Council considered it too expensive, and in 1977 the City Engineer's Department and Parks Department laid out a new park themselves.

In 1983 there was a short-lived proposal to create an underground shopping centre underneath Castle Park, but it came to nothing.

A major programme of improvements was carried out in 1991-93 with money provided by the developers of The Galleries shopping centre in return for allowing part of it to be used as a temporary open-air car park. It was formally opened by the Lord Mayor once more on May 19 1993.

More than 70 years after the Blitz, Castle Park remains one of the greatest unresolved problems of Bristol's built environment. The former financial buildings next to the bridge are derelict, while behind them the ruins of St Mary-le-Port church, left in place as a memorial to those who died, are overgrown and covered in graffiti.

In 2006 Bristol firm Deeley Freed came up with a plan for the site; a 'mixed use' development of offices, shops and flats. Bristol City Council, which owns the land, was behind the plan, but because it would involve taking up some more of what was now established parkland it met with furious opposition. Interestingly, the first people to object tended to be office workers who use the Park during their lunch-hours in good weather. More than 5,000 people signed a petition opposing the development.

Proposals were batted to and fro. Employing two public relations firms, Deeley Freed staged an exhibition of its proposals, and offered to 'release' some money to the Council to improve what was left of Castle Park once the deal was signed. Meanwhile, campaigners launched a bid to save the Park from development by applying to have it registered as a Town Green. The planning inspector rejected the application.

The recession has now put paid to the St Mary-le-Port plans, and the Council's agreement with Deeley Freed has lapsed. Sooner or later there will be new proposals for this embarrassing eyesore.

The City of Frampton Cotterell 1966-1973

One of the preoccupations of Britain's government in the 1960s was the growth of South-East England. The country was getting lopsided in terms of population and jobs, so Whitehall made several attempts to shift people and workplaces away from London and the Home Counties and into the regions.

Since the end of the war, Britain had been building new towns, initially around London itself (e.g. Stevenage, Basildon), and by now further afield as well (e.g. Aycliffe, East Kilbride). An alarming projection in population figures suggesting that there might be 70 million people living in Britain by 2000 now prompted the government to consider not just new towns, but new cities – places which would have a million or more inhabitants by the end of the century.

In July 1966 George Brown, the Minister for Economic Affairs, announced that the government was looking into three potential new cities, to be sited on the estuaries of the Tay, Humber and Severn. Each, he said, would contain a transport hub to and from which people might travel by car, rail or monorail. Inside each complex there would be moving walkways, escalators and electric vehicles for passengers and luggage.

Studies were commissioned and carried out. The one for 'Severnside', as it was now being called, said that the area could accommodate a massive increase in population, and that this could be done via extending Bristol and Newport, and with a cluster of new towns in Gloucestershire. A lot of this expansion could be concentrated in the Bristol/Bath region by building a massive new development centred on Frampton Cotterell. With up to 300,000 inhabitants by the year 2000, Frampton Cotterell would be three quarters the size of Bristol and four times bigger than Bath.

The idea was discussed sporadically – a lot of people living in rural Gloucestershire were understandably alarmed – until it was formally abandoned in April 1973. Environment Secretary Geoffrey Rippon told the Commons that earlier forecasts of Britain's population reaching 70 million by 2000 were probably wrong; the number would more likely be around 61 million (which turned out to be correct). The Minister said that the new cities would have required a massive national effort, but now it seemed possible to provide for the lesser numbers through the controlled growth of existing urban areas, or new towns.

Of course since then we have seen huge amounts of housing and commercial development to the north of Bristol – at Cribbs Causeway, Stoke Gifford, Bradley Stoke, Patchway and more. But no new Severnside City. Frampton Cotterell remains a village with a parish council. For now.

Pathways in the Air 1966-1973

In the mid-1960s, the rest of the world was getting closer to Bristol – and it would be arriving by car. The completion of the new motorways to London and the Midlands, and the opening of the new Severn Bridge made Bristol look like an attractive regional location for offices and warehousing. All the more so when the government took measures to discourage office developments in London and the South East and move them elsewhere in the country. From the late 1960s onwards, several finance and insurance companies did indeed relocate to Bristol, with its excellent communications, lower rents and plentiful office space.

In 1966 the City Planning Department, as part of a periodic review of a city development plan originally drawn up in 1952, produced a new 'City Centre Policy Report' which advocated a traffic policy which now seems quite remarkable.

Assuming that whatever happens in America comes to Britain sooner or later, planners looked at the way in which the huge growth of car ownership and car-based commuting in the USA had turned many American city centres into wastelands dominated by huge, noisy roads.

The Bristol vision was indeed to build big roads, and to keep the traffic moving, but it aimed to maintain life on a human scale in the centre of town. It would do this with a network of aerial walkways and plazas where people could wander at their leisure, while the traffic thundered past down below.

This was not a particularly new idea. In 1959, the Bristol Architects Forum, the Young Turks at the Royal West of England Academy who were out to challenge the local old guard, published a document called *A Plan for Bristol*. Among other things this had proposed a pedestrian deck and 'Venetian piazza' over the Centre.

The pedestrian decks tend to be ignored in accounts of this period, as campaigners against aspects of the City Centre Policy Report and the development plan review focussed on the huge growth in road-building they anticipated, and this in turn fed into objections to the Outer Ring Road and plans to cover over/fill in parts of the docks.

Putting pedestrians in the sky seemed like a visionary and brilliant idea. Imagine a system covering central Bristol, from Lewins Mead to College Green. It would go up as far as Park Row, taking in the newly-opened New Bristol Centre, where they had a cinema, ballroom and an ice rink. There would be walkways across the centre, and a piazza over the Centre. You could walk from the Bristol & West Building (as was – it's now the Radisson Blu Hotel) or the Colston Hall, as far as Broadmead without encountering any cars or having to cross a road.

Your route would not merely take you over bridges;

The 1950 Forum Plan for Bristol demonstrated, amongst other things, how the then incomplete Inner Ring Road would operate more efficiently if it were made one-way. This drawing by Mike Jenner shows his design for the decked-over city centre. Courtesy Mike Jenner) ▶

for much of your journey you would be going along sidewalks next to the first or second floors of new office buildings and apartment blocks. There would be shops, pubs and cafés, too. You could buy your newspaper and a pack of Woodbines as you went, perhaps stopping also for a cup of tea and a fried egg sandwich, or maybe visit a milk bar. Welcome to the swinging sixties, Bristol-style!

This was never going to be an easy dream to realise, but by the late 60s, Bristol was in the middle of a major property boom, with new speculative office developments springing up everywhere. In 1970 the Council acquired some land fronting onto St Augustines Parade and was hoping that the centre-piece of its vision could be put in place. On this side there was talk of an opera house and a new theatre; three bridges and the central

piazza (opposite the entrance to Baldwin Street) would link to the first storey of the new Bristol & West Tower, and most/all of it would be paid for by developers who would have to put their part of the pedestrian decking jigsaw into place if they wanted a piece of Bristol's booming market.

So much for the theory.

The original vision for homes as well as shops was consistently watered down as developers lobbied the Council for single-use office blocks. Plans in 1971 to fence off all the roads in the centre and Lewins Mead (once the decks were all in place) were attacked furiously by citizen groups as a measure which would deter people from walking in the centre at all.

The Council did what councils so often do when confronted with controversy; they called in some

There are a few traces of the pedestrian decking system that never was, such as the walkways and sidewalks over Nelson Street and Rupert Street

consultants. Ove, Arup and Partners were not encouraging. The firm's report said the scheme would increase the amount of traffic moving through the city, along with the noise and the pollution. More to the point, it probably wouldn't move any faster. It also wondered if the shops and other businesses on the decks would ever be sufficiently profitable to attract tenants.

In 1972, announcing that footbridges were to be built crossing Nelson Street and Rupert Street, the Council also let it be known that no more were planned, and the whole scheme was allowed to die quietly. At the end of the following year, the property market across the country collapsed dramatically, and Bristol found itself oversupplied with new concrete office blocks. There would be no big piazza in the sky for the Centre. It would remain two big traffic islands with a couple of litter-strewn municipal flower beds for years to come.

There are some parts of Bristol where the system was put in place, and where vestiges of it can be seen. One is the former Bristol & West Building, but the best place is St John's Court, aka National Westminster Court. This was a development completed by Legal & General in 1972, and includes the previously mentioned footbridges over Nelson and Rupert Streets. There's even one of the fabled piazzas, now rather windswept, on top of Froomsgate House, and another on the Whitefriars Building, which seems to have been gated off. Nobody ever uses them.

Central Telephone Exchange

1967-1972

Just as London got its own Post Office Tower (nowadays the BT Tower) in 1965, Bristol was due to get one as well. This would house a telephone exchange and microwave aerials as well as offices.

Discussions began between the Post Office (which ran the phone system in those days) and Bristol's planning officials in 1967. The initial proposal was for a block with two towers on its site near Welsh Back.

At this time certain statutory bodies, such as the Post Office, were expected to respect the wishes of local planning authorities, but in theory they had the powers to override any objections if they wished. In this case, the planners objected to twin towers and so the Post Office went back to the drawing board.

Various designs were looked at and consulted on, and in 1971 it came back with plans for a huge 305ft single tower. This would have been half as high again as the new Bristol & West tower, four times as wide, and 100ft higher than the tallest commercial structure in Bristol, the DRG building just across Bristol Bridge.

This sparked an immediate campaign from people who felt it would be inelegant and completely inappropriate for its setting. It would loom over the historic streets of Welsh Back, Queen Square and King Street, said objectors. One small but particularly effective episode was the publication in the *Evening Post* of a letter, accompanied by a simple line-drawing of the massive bulk of the proposed building dwarfing King Street and the Theatre Royal.

The drawing was by Jerry Hicks, a local art teacher

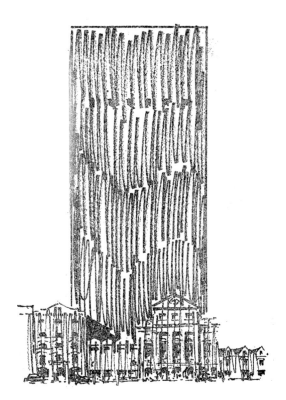

▲ Jerry Hicks' drawing of the GPO building, showing how it would loom over the Theatre Royal on King Street

and Civic Society activist; in an article in *Architectural Design* magazine he satirised the design as part of a sinister plot to make Bristol as terrible a place to live in as possible:

The destruction [of King Street] will be achieved visually by dwarfing its scale to a point where it appears ridiculous. Immediately behind the Theatre Royal...will loom a gigantic edifice hundreds of feet high full of GPO machinery and 16 men. This grotesque up-ending of a mountain of possibly obsolete machinery in the heart of the city should be a fitting climax to the central devastation.

To ram home the point, the campaigners talked of flying a barrage balloon at 300ft over the site so that passing Bristolians would see exactly how tall it was going to be. The design was rejected by the Council's Planning Committee and in April 1972 the Post Office announced the project would be abandoned. Instead it would construct a building only 90ft high, with six floors instead of the original 20.

The Grand Spa Hotel 1969-1973

The Grand Spa Hotel, nowadays the Avon Gorge Hotel, wanted to build an extension onto its front. This alarmed a wide range of people who thought that it would be a monstrous carbuncle on the natural beauty of the Gorge.

Of all the Bristol schemes which public opinion mobilised to prevent, the saga of the hotel is probably the most colourful and dramatic. It is understandably deeply ingrained in the mythology both of the Bristol Civic Society, and of the Clifton & Hotwells Improvement Society.

The Grand Hotel Co (Bristol) was in discussion with the Council about its plans to build an extension to the Grand Spa Hotel in late 1969, but the news only became public in January 1971. The company, with the help of planners on the Council, appeared to be moving with indecent haste.

This breathtaking speed by the normally glacial standards of town hall bureaucracy was down to money. The English Tourist Board was making grants of up to £1,000 per room available for new hotel developments, but these had to be taken up within a few months.

The company registered a planning application for an extension to the existing building – in effect a whole new building – with 126 double rooms, a few single rooms, car parking for 203 vehicles and banqueting facilities for 250 covers. The building would be eight storeys and 30 metres high, 80 metres long and 180 metres from the Clifton tower of the Suspension Bridge.

The Clifton & Hotwells Improvement Society, which had been formed in 1968 and whose membership included large numbers of young professional people who had been gentrifying the area for some years, moved to set up an action group called STAG – Save The Avon Gorge.

By the time the Planning Committee met on January 27, the Council had received 174 letters of objection; nonetheless outline planning approval was granted. A later Civic Society account of the episode says:

In 1971 both the Labour and Conservative parties in Bristol stood firmly and defensively against the amenity societies whose informed criticisim's of the City's post-war planning and architecture record seemed damaging to political reputations.

Soon after the meeting, objections to the plan were coming from all over the country. The Avon Gorge had become more than just a parochial issue. This prompted STAG to switch focus from the Council,

A worm's eye view ... ▶ Objectors to the hotel development said it was essential to look at architect's models from below, not above, to get a full appreciation of its visual impact on the Avon Gorge

which was looking like a lost cause, to central government. It encouraged objectors to write to the Secretary of State at the newly-formed Department of the Environment.

Mail deliveries were unreliable due to industrial action by postal workers, but STAG managed to turn this to its advantage by organising its own delivery service, with couriers collecting letters dropped at a number of locations in London, and taking them to the Department of the Environment every second day. The Minister, Peter Walker, would eventually find around 1,200 letters in his in-tray.

At the same time, though, the Planning Committee was about to meet to consider drawings submitted by the developer. The Council feared a hefty compensation bill from the developers if the project did not proceed. Just a few hours before the meeting, which would almost certainly have granted full permission to the development, a phone call from Whitehall 'called in' the drawings.

In the second half of May, a public inquiry took place. It ran for nine days and was covered by the national media.

The STAG case against the development was based on the visual impact of the building, and its likely effect on the environment. The objectors' case was led by the formidable Paul Chadd QC, who normally worked as a criminal barrister. 'He treated people the same way that he would cross-examine criminals in the dock,' said one witness later.

Jerry Hicks, one of the campaigners, made the point that looking at an architect's model of the hotel in its setting was misleading as one's perspective is from above. What people needed to do, he said, was try and grasp its visual impact from ground level. For that purpose he ran pieces of string to parts of the model hotel and invited them to crouch on the floor to get some idea of how it would look from ground level.

Witnesses called by the objectors included architects, botanists, the editor of the *Architectural Review* and, most famous of all, Sir John Betjeman, poet, author, architecture-lover and national treasure. Professor Desmond Donovan, head of the geology department at University College London, told the inquiry that there was every reason to believe that during the construction phase rainwater might well cause landslides on the edge of the Gorge. The heads of neighbouring councils on the Somerset side objected to the plan, which they had first heard about from newspaper reports.

The Ministry Inspector recommended that the building should not be approved.

The fallout was messy. The company hit the Council with a compensation claim for £251,000, while the Council said that the Department of the Environment should face at least some of the liability.

The following year the firm came back with a new application for a smaller building, around half the size of the first proposal. The Council now said that since the Environment Secretary had taken the original decision out of its hands, he should rule on this one as well. The new minister, Geoffrey Rippon, ordered a new inquiry, scheduled for June 1973. Now, however, with inflation rising and the firm not knowing when or if it would ever be allowed to proceed, it was announced in May that they were abandoning the project.

Filling in the Docks 1969-1975

One of the things that most Bristolians interested in local affairs 'know' is that at some point in the 1960s or 1970s, the Council had an insane scheme to fill in the City Docks and cover them with roads and offices – or something. This lives in local folklore as an act of stupendous folly which could have deprived the city of one of its greatest assets, and which was only prevented by vigorous protest action by concerned citizens.

The myth is substantially accurate. It might even be argued that this was the single most important episode in Bristol's post-war history, since it ensured that the 83 football pitches' worth of water in the heart of the city would play a key role in the regeneration of the central area. It also played its part in changing politics at the Council House.

The struggle for the future of the docks overlaps with, and was linked to, the Council's ambitious road-building programme.

The 1947 Town & Country Planning Act obliged Bristol to produce a 'development plan' which was published in 1952. This plan was meant to be reviewed and revised every five years or so, and to the 1966 review was added a new City Centre Policy Report laying down guidelines for the future shape of the central areas. Neither document had much to say about the Docks.

They did, however, anticipate that more and more people would be commuting into the city to work in offices already there, and offices yet to be built. Car ownership in Bristol had doubled between 1950 and 1961, and the amount of road traffic was bound to increase. The need to improve the road system was growing more urgent.

Part of the solution was the proposed pedestrian decking system (see 'Pathways in the Air', earlier), and the rest of it lay in completing inner and outer circuit roads.

The Council's roadbuilding mania seems bizarre in an age where we at least pay lip-service to the idea of public transport as being better than private cars, but things were different in the 1960s. Widening car-ownership was seen as progressive and democratic, a privilege and convenience percolating down the social classes. Public transport, most people believed, was for life's losers.

The problem was that not everyone wanted roads in their neighbourhood, or on beauty spots. In March 1967 a public inquiry was held into Council proposals to build a huge roundabout on the Downs, at the top of Blackboy Hill. Despite many local objections, this scheme was approved, but was never built due to a legal technicality over the need for a compensating land transfer to make up for the loss of the open space.

At the same time an inquiry was being conducted into the development plan review, with most public objections focussed on the Outer Circuit Road. The inquiry accepted the plan, with some modifications,

▲ Too many cars, too many ring roads. Jerry Hicks' cartoon

but suggested a three-year cooling-off period before any substantial work was done. The game changed dramatically in 1969 when Bristol City Council announced its intention to close the City Docks.

The harbour had been the heart of Bristol's life more or less since the city's very foundation, but now it was no longer a commercial proposition. The City Docks were now handling only something like 10% of Bristol's total cargo, while the rest went to Avonmouth. In 1970 this would still amount to 800,000 tons, but fewer and fewer ships were coming up the river. Within just a few years the number of ships berthing each day in the Floating Harbour had gone from an average of three to less than one.

Technology was changing, too, with the increasing move of maritime freight to containers, which the City Docks were not equipped to handle. And of course there was the age-old problem of getting large vessels up and down the river.

The Council was also confident that it would get the government go-ahead for its planned new West Dock at Avonmouth, which would indeed open as Royal Portbury Dock in 1977.

By 1969 the City Docks were losing money. At the same time, it was also thought that Harold Wilson's Labour government was on the verge of nationalising most or all of the country's docks. To lose control of a huge part of the central area of the city would have been anathema to a town hall of any political complexion. There was an urgent need to close the docks to stay ahead of any likely government land-grab, though in the end this never materialised.

From the planners' viewpoint, dock closure had a great advantage; it would make completing the new road system easier. Large stretches of water right in the middle of the city could now be covered over or filled in to provide space for roads and offices. Where the water remained, bridges could be built more cheaply as they would no longer have to be high enough to provide clearance for ships.

The Council's *Bristol Civic News* announced in August 1969 that it was promoting a Parliamentary Bill enabling the city to withdraw navigation rights from the Docks. The article spoke of bringing in a 'lagoon system', which was a way of saying there would still be stretches of water in the middle of the city, and an even nicer way of saying other stretches would disappear.

Objectors to the plan claimed that putting the news out in August, when so many people were away on holiday, was a sneaky ploy by the Council to prevent protest. If so, it didn't work. The Civic Society, the Clifton & Hotwells Improvement Society, the Cabot Cruising Club and the local branch of the Inland Waterways Association immediately mobilised.

At a town meeting at the Colston Hall that December, attendees on the electoral register voted overwhelmingly to oppose the Bill. As the debate hotted up, the Council held a local referendum, waging a major PR campaign to win over public support. Among other things, it claimed that the Bill was essential if Bristol was to secure the future of the docks for amenity purposes. Some 22,298 ratepayers voted in favour of the Bill, with 16,724 against.

The Bristol Corporation Bill went off to Parliament and was passed in 1971. It gave the Council all the powers it needed to close and reclaim parts of the Harbour, though amendments had been gained preventing any reduction in the amount of water surface – therefore earlier fears about stretches being covered over or filled in were allayed to some degree. Another amendment preserved the navigation rights of small craft in the docks.

The provisions of the bill were to take effect in 1980, and so now Bristol entered a prolonged period of debate about the future.

Casson, Conder & Partners were appointed to study the replanning of the Docks. The consultants' brief was to come up with advice on how best to use the various areas around the Floating Harbour, provided there were three low fixed bridges for motorways.

The *Bristol City Docks Redevelopment Study*, delivered in 1972, is a fairly short, and quite remarkable document. The 'Casson Report', as it became known, contained no glossy pictures and few tables of figures

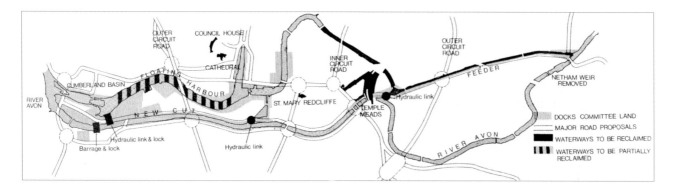

▲ The plan for the City Docks, as it first appeared in *Bristol Civic News*, August 1969

and statistics. Instead its tone is rather idealistic, even poetic in places. It dutifully included the roads and bridges, but its comments on the proposed road system, and its map showing where these would fall, cannot have pleased anyone down at the Council House. It merits a lengthy quote:

Here we have a shining wedge of water bounded by romantically dilapidated wharves and robust warehouses driven into the very centre of the city, and now facing a new and useful future. Obviously this future cannot be left to chance. Nor, so rich is the area's potential variety of form and mood, should it be too strictly regimented. The clean sweep and the imposed formula would be as socially and aesthetically unwelcome as the architectural bedlam of private initiative taking what chances it can.

So a plan there must be – or more accurately, an attitude of mind. Facts, statistics and graphs, regulations and controls are useful, but they are no substitute for imagination. Those who govern the City and those who elect them must be in partnership, inspired by an 'idea'. Obviously the aim is a good environment, space without waste, compactness without congestion, architectural character and natural advantages everywhere sought out, identified, conserved, and, where possible, enriched.

... The waters of the harbour, used to unify and to separate, to enliven and relax – should return to the citizens for their enjoyment: the wharves and banks to be opened up for boatyards, marinas and waterside promenades with the restored *Great Britain* as the magnificent centrepiece.

The report also said that the Outer Circuit Road crossing the Floating Harbour was an idea that should be 'most seriously re-considered'. An urban motorway on the scale that the city proposed would cause 'very great disturbance' to the unique character of the docks.

It went on to examine each of the different neighbourhoods around the Harbour, looking at how they could be used anew. Recommendations for what developers and planners nowadays called 'mixed use'

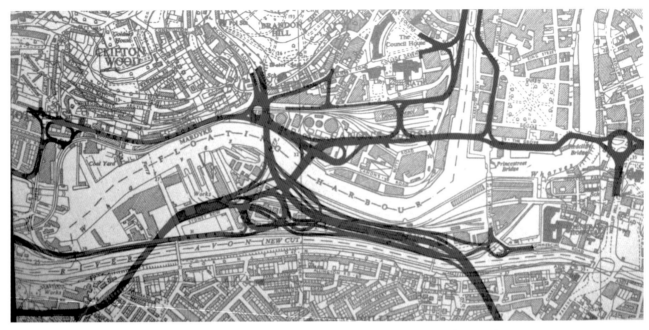

▲ Map from the Casson Report, showing all possible road schemes and how they would affect the Docks

– residential, commercial, leisure, etc. – were by the standards of the time quite radical.

Opponents of the Council plans meanwhile formed a City Docks Group to look at alternative uses for the area. The Group's membership drew on the increasingly powerful amenity societies, and included several professional people, including architects, engineers and lawyers. It had a broad and highly-motivated pool of expertise and creative talent to draw on – all free of charge. The series of reports it produced between 1973 and 1977 looking at the future use of the area could not be ignored by the Council. Essentially these fleshed out the Casson Report with suggestions for low-rise, high-density housing, a sympathetic integration of old and new buildings, and making maximum use of the water both as a backdrop and for leisure activities.

At one point it was even suggested that the main campus of the new Bristol Polytechnic (nowadays the University of the West of England) should have a dockside site.

To this day, the amenity societies and individual campaigners claim that their lobbying played a key part in saving the docks from destruction, and in the subsequent shaping of the modern area.

Up to a point ... Other factors were in play by 1973-74. Collapsing property values, inflation, the OPEC oil crisis and domestic political instability meant that the sort of government capital funding needed for the road system was unlikely to materialise.

BRISTOL & WEST TOWER

The Bristol & West Tower, built in 1967/68, would have played a key part in the pedestrian decking system, anchoring it on the eastern side.

When the firm relocated to Temple Quay in 2000 new owners Grosvenor Estates said they were looking at various options for the site. Most of these involved demolishing the old building. They decided they'd like to replace it with a taller, slimmer building with apartments at the top, offices below them, and shops and restaurants at the bottom.

The design by Alec French Architects – who were also responsible for the 1960s building – was praised by the Commission for Architecture & the Built Environment's design panel, but proved controversial with some people who felt that it was too tall for such a central location.

Despite enthusiasm from officials, it was voted down by the Planning Committee (Central) by five votes to four. The development had now been taken over by Crosby Homes, who decided against submitting a new design.

The building was left standing. It was clad in blue glass and is now a hotel.

(Pictures: Alec French Architects and Stephen Morris)

Local politics also played a part. Until now, the Council's Labour group had been an enthusiastic supporter of new development, but the mood was changing. Many councillors were beginning to realise what impact the roads would have on the communities in their wards, and they didn't like it. By the time of the 1973 local elections, Labour had swung decisively against the circuit roads, and against office developments. Many on the Labour side linked the over-supply of office space in the city to a shortage of housing and the decline of manufacturing employment.

So while the rebellion against concreting over the docks was often led by the professionals in the amenity societies, it would be a mistake to see this as a purely middle-class movement. The local press, particularly the *Evening Post*, gave huge amounts of coverage to the issue, and for many Bristolians, even if they would not be directly affected by new roads, the destruction of the docks, with it centuries of heritage, was a powerfully emotive issue. One of the biggest crowds ever seen in Bristol had turned out to watch the return of Brunel's ss *Great Britain* to the docks in July 1970 – an estimated 200,000 people had lined the banks of the Avon, or stood on the Suspension Bridge, to watch her come up the river and lock in at Cumberland Basin following her epic voyage back from the Falklands.

She was later moved to the Great Western Dockyard, which now faced the threat of a motorway running next to it.

In the elections, which unusually were for the whole Council, Labour retained control with a significantly increased majority.

But something else happened as well; for the first time since 1926 there were Liberals on the Council. Three new Liberal members had been elected. One was George Ferguson, who would become Bristol's first elected mayor 39 years later.

The Liberals had been an increasingly convincing local political presence in recent years, but this was their first electoral breakthrough, and they had campaigned almost entirely on the issues of planning and redevelopment. A Liberal spokesman, writing in the local press days before the polls, said:

Bristol is a unique city. It needs PROTECTING against powerful interests that threaten to replace familiar streets and views with over-sized roads, offices and car parks. It needs IMPROVING by the clearance and imaginative use of derelict sites as gardens, playgrounds and low-cost housing.

In that sense, you might say that the Liberal Party in Bristol in 1973 was seen as the political wing of the Civic Society, the Clifton & Hotwells Improvement Society, and other amenity societies in middle-class neighbourhoods. The Liberals, later Liberal Democrats, had started their long march to eventually taking power in the Council House decades later.

Pressure for road-building over the docks had more or less evaporated by the time the new county of Avon took over responsibility for highways in April 1974. Some damage had been done by then, notably the demolition of 550 houses in Totterdown for a never-to-be-built huge roundabout/junction.

Many Bristol Council officers working in transport planning went to Avon as a career move. There would now also be tensions between the two authorities; one short-term political gain for Labour-run Bristol was that it could now criticise (usually Tory-run) Avon's transport plans with impunity. Bristol now joined forces with the civic and residents' organisations to campaign against two road bridges which had been key elements in the Outer Ring Road. One would have run across the end of St Augustine's Reach, right next to the Arnolfini. The other would have crossed the Harbour at the bottom of Jacobs Wells Road, landing on the other side right next to where the Great Britain was now berthed.

The ring road plans were eventually cancelled, though there has been plenty more road-building since... Meanwhile, Bristol put a temporary freeze on all new office developments, but thanks to the country's wider economic woes, there would be no new major local developments until the end of the 1970s anyway. If you wander the streets of Bristol now you'll find almost no building of any size or importance built between 1973 and 1980.

The Council-owned Port of Bristol Authority handed responsibility for the City Docks over to the Council on April 1 1975 and city officials recommended abandoning the 1971 Act (which they did the following year). In 1975 the city also finally agreed that the *Great Britain* should have the right to remain in the docks permanently. The Arnolfini, which many like to claim led the reinvention of the docks, moved into the Bush warehouse in 1975 as an art gallery and restaurant. A cinema showing mostly foreign-language art films would be added later.

The amenity groups did less to save the docks than the global economy and Bristol's Labour group, but with their armies of experts and their sophisticated campaigning techniques they had run rings around overworked planning officials and councillors, and won the argument hands-down. They had set the agenda for the future regeneration of the Docks, and while there would be plenty of rows in the years to come, everyone had signed up for their vision of how to move forward. And most people would agree that, barring a few failures here and there, it has been a great success.

20 Ideas for Bristol 1975 & 1976

The 1960s and 70s rebellion against concrete and big, brutal buildings found a more playful and fun outlet in exhibitions run over two consecutive years at the Bristol City Museum & Art Gallery.

'Twenty Ideas for Bristol' (subtitle: 'Ideas for improving a city's life and environment') showcased suggestions put forward by people in their 20s and 30s, including architects, engineers, artists, musicians and schoolteachers.

'There was no vision of the city really, other than of a city of transport and commercial development' said one of the organisers, architect Richard Lee in an interview many years later.

There was nothing about people living in it. And Bristol had a wonderful collection of Georgian and Victorian buildings in brick and stone, and what they wanted to do was tear them down and replace them with modern buildings of glass and concrete.

So we thought we should mount an exhibition of ideas, and hopefully this would sow the seeds of ideas that would go on to flourish in other ways. And a lot of things that have happened since are partly a result of the seeds that were sown at that time.

The ideas ranged from the commonsense to the ridiculous, from the costly to the cost-free ... though with most falling somewhere in between. Everyone loved the idea of the ticket barrier on the Suspension Bridge taking the form of a life-size statue of Brunel, mechanically raising his stovepipe hat as he lets you through. Peter Lawrence, who came up with this idea, also picked up on Brunel's original Egyptian-themed design for the bridge and suggested hanging a pair of giant curtains from the Bridge painted to make the Avon look like the Nile, complete with surrounding desert, pyramids and palm trees.

There was a fabulous scheme to have a funicular railway up Marlborough Hill – this is the steep street that runs from near the Bristol Royal Infirmary up to Kingsdown. The railway would be a quick and

▲ Pete Lawrence, *Curtain Drawn Across the Gorge*, 1975. (Bristol's Museums, Galleries & Archives)

Pete Lawrence, *Brunel Takes His Hat Off to the Passing Motorist*, 1975. (Bristol's Museums, Galleries & Archives)
◄

BLUE WAVE

In 2011 a local company named Wave-garden UK announced it was seeking to build Britain's first inland 'surfing experience' at the 13-acre former Bristol & West sports ground on the Portway next to the Avon. Using technology developed in Spain, the facility would create artificial waves for surfing. The plans ran into some opposition from nearby residents and conservationists, but the company, now called The Wave: Bristol, announced at the end of 2012 that it was looking at other, larger sites in the Bristol area. Advances in the wave technology meant the project had now outgrown the Portway site and the team needed to look elsewhere to 'create a sustainable attraction where people of all backgrounds and abilities can learn to surf and get in touch with nature.'

▲ Adrian Jones, *Bristol Folly: A Way of Recycling Threatened Buildings.* (Bristol's Museums, Galleries & Archives)

painless way of getting from the city centre to Cotham and the design for the railway car included racking for bikes and prams.

Another suggestion was for the Portway to be closed to traffic every Sunday so that cyclists and pedestrians could enjoy the Avon Gorge in safety and peace and quiet.

Some of the 40 ideas would eventually be realised in one form or another. A proposal for a city farm, for instance. There were also suggestions for cycle paths and traffic-free neighbourhoods.

One of the contributors was architect George Ferguson, who proposed putting the statue of Queen Victoria on College Green into the middle of a maze, or draining the moat in front of the Council House to turn it into a winter garden and butterfly sanctuary.

'At the time we were thinking that we should look around for ways to cheer Bristol up,' he said later. 'That was the great thing about '20 Ideas' – there were loads of very cheerful ones. It was all very much on a human scale, looking at things from the viewpoint of the individual and not about how we build higher buildings or bigger motorway junctions.'

200 Ideas for Bristol 2006

As part of the bicentenary celebrations of Brunel's birth, the Bristol Cultural Development Partnership decided to celebrate Bristolian inventiveness with an update of the 1970s exhibitions. The public, invited to send in ideas, duly submitted over 400 suggestions, and some of the best of these were showcased at an exhibition at Bristol's Architecture Centre.

Built with pedestrians and horse-drawn carriages and carts in mind, the Clifton Suspension Bridge nowadays takes thousands of motor vehicles daily. Bristol's Aedas Architects Ltd entered this design for the 200 Ideas for Bristol exhibition. Aedas' concept was 'to provide a new dynamic structure beneath the existing bridge for vehicles and to fully pedestrianise the suspension bridge above.' It was never intended to be actually built ... (Aedas Architects Ltd) ▼

▲ Concorde model in the Centre, idea by Alana Gordon for 200 Ideas for Bristol. (Bristol Cultural Development Partnership)

The winner was a proposal to install Redcliffe sandstone blocks topped with stainless steel mirrors in Corn Street to encourage people to look upwards at the sky and the surrounding buildings.

Other popular suggestions included a huge Mount Rushmore-style carving of Brunel's face in the Avon Gorge, a hot air balloon museum at Ashton Court, a full-size model of Concorde in the Centre, and a bike lift up Park Street.

▲ Brunel effigy in the Avon Gorge – proposed by Alan
Trimby, illustrated by Simon Gurr for 200 Ideas for Bristol.
(Bristol Cultural Development Partnership)

The Avon Metro (and its descendants) 1979-present

Late on the night of April 11 1941, a German bomb destroyed the St Philips Bridge and cut the main power cable from the Bristol Tramways power station.

There was only one tram out that night, the last evening service from Old Market to Kingswood. The lights on the car crewed by Driver Webster and Conductor Brittan flickered, then died, and their machine ground to a standstill.

The tramcar had stopped at the top of a slope. They asked some bystanders for a push, and freewheeled the car into the Kingswood depot. Thus ended the last journey in the 65-year history of Bristol's tram system.

While we might nowadays regard the loss of Bristol's trams with nostalgia or regret, they were little mourned at the time. By the 1930s the trams were regarded as old-fashioned and uncomfortable, not least because their top decks were open to the elements. The company was also a local byword for atrocious industrial relations, with frequent strikes and a notoriously reactionary management.

Bristol's Council had finally invoked an old contractual right to buy the company, and was now closing down lines and replacing trams with newfangled motor buses. When the last tram to Horfield depot left the Centre on July 15 1939, a crowd gathered to watch and to sing 'Auld Lang Syne'. This was slightly more genteel than the previous year, when the last tram to Staple Hill had been torn to pieces by souvenir-hunters.

The German bomb had only hastened the inevitable. It would be over 40 years before most Bristolians seriously considered the possibility of a new tram system.

The Avon Metro was the brainchild of architect Brian Tucker and Richard Cottrell, the Conservative MEP for Bristol (when the city was a separate Euro constituency). The pair had first proposed the idea in the late 1970s, and initially it was loosely modelled on the Tyne & Wear Metro. It would have used some local British Rail track, while the central section of Bristol was to have been underground. Even if such a plan had secured the support of both Bristol and Avon councils, the costs would have been considerable.

As the 1980s progressed, a more realistic plan emerged, and one more in keeping with the new spirit of the times. A company called Advanced Transport for Avon (ATA) was formed to create a new tram (or strictly speaking, light rapid transit) network which would connect the centre of Bristol to surrounding towns. Some new rails would have to be laid in the centre of Bristol, but for the most part the system would use existing or redundant rail routes.

The Avon Metro, or the '£230m Avon Metro' as the local media dubbed it, would, claimed ATA, be financed by the private sector. Cottrell, a colourful and extrovert front-man who had previously been a TV presenter, said it would not cost ratepayers or taxpayers any money. In a phrase which would later haunt the project, he called it 'a free gift to the people of Avon.'

The scheme was unveiled to the public and press amid a great deal of fanfare in November 1987. Before the century was out, Bristol would have a clean and efficient network of state-of-the-art trams each whisking up to 200 passengers at a time into town and home again.

The first route, from Wapping Wharf in the city centre to Portishead and Portbury, was due to open by 1991, and the entire system would be completed by the late 90s.

Subsequent routes would include:

· City centre to Yate via Temple Meads, North East Bristol and Emersons Green, with the potential for an interchange link with the M4.

· City Centre to Filton via Temple Meads, Parkway and Bradley Stoke.

· City Centre to South Bristol, with one fork terminating at Hartcliffe, and another going off to Weston-super-Mare.

The model had now switched from the Tyne & Wear Metro to that of London's Docklands Light Railway, which had partly been built by private enterprise. A bill was put before Parliament applying for permission for the first line to Portishead, out along the Avon Gorge. 'A route which passes sites fat with development potential,' noted *The Times*, approvingly.

This would be the key to financing the scheme, company secretary Jack Penrose told *The Times*.

This is a private enterprise project. The first major asset the company will have is the parliamentary bill. Once we have that we expect to raise money from the increase in land values resulting from

▲ Richard Cottrell at the Advanced Transport for Avon project launch, November 1987. (*Bristol Post*)

the rail transit.

While the financial model seemed new and daring in the 1980s, ATA's own publicity material was quick to point out that more or less all of Britain's rail network had been built by private companies during the Victorian era. In the bullish financial atmosphere of the mid-1980s, the stock market was booming, property

▲ Artist's impression of an Avon Metro tram produced for Advanced Transport for Avon, 1987. (*Bristol Post*)

prices were on the rise, and on the edge of Bristol, building work on the vast new suburb of Bradley Stoke was under way. The scheme seemed perfectly feasible.

The Parliamentary bill for the first route received Royal Assent in May 1989 but even by then it was running into problems. The Port of Bristol was concerned that the Metro would block it from fully exploiting the freight potential of a reopened line from Portbury into Bristol. ATA was also starting to find that there was no easy way for it to take any share

in the increased value of land around the lines that was owned by other developers.

There was an even bigger problem with politics. The aggressively Thatcherite tone of some of ATA's supporters grated with left-wingers and trade unionists. Bristol South MP Dawn Primarolo raised concerns about the system's safety and financing in the Commons. Bristol's Labour-controlled Council was also opposed to aspects of the company's second bill, to run a link from the Floating Harbour to

Temple Meads via the Centre. It was rejected in the Lords, though in the meantime the Labour group's deputy leader resigned after his colleagues refused to allow his suggested compromises which would have allowed the plan to go ahead.

A third Bill, which was going to run part of two routes along the old Midland Railway line, was later withdrawn following objections from users of the cyclepath, and the Bitton steam railway.

By late 1991, ATA was in trouble. The economic downturn made it difficult to raise finance. A bid to raise funding in Europe came to nothing. Later hints to the media about some vast fund of money from the Middle East came to nothing. Any anticipated gains from rising land values had also evaporated. Despite this, Avon County Council was still supportive, and even seconding staff to ATA's offices.

At this point, the newly-privatised local bus company Badgerline, which was also a shareholder in ATA, was starting to experiment with new transport forms of its own. Guided Light Transit (GLT) vehicles, powered by overhead cables and guided by a single rail in the road, could also convert to manually-driven diesel buses where the infrastructure did not exist. GLT seemed like a more flexible solution to Bristol's transport problems. The first route Badgerline considered did not threaten ATA, but when it started looking into running a GLT route to Bradley Stoke, it looked like head-on competition. Because Badgerline would also want local or central government funding, this was bound to dilute ATA's bid for taxpayer cash.

Now the creditors were at the door. ATA's consulting engineers, who were owed over £400,000,

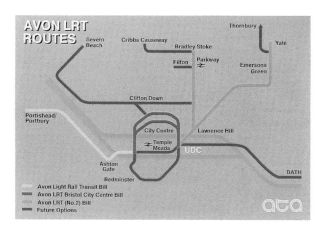

▲ Advanced Transport for Avon's proposed tram routes.
(*Bristol Post*)

petitioned for ATA's liquidation. It was wound up in the High Court in March 1992 with debts of £3.8m. Its parent company, Advanced Transport Projects, was dissolved later that year because it had failed to file accounts. Its debts were alleged to be a further £1m.

By now, Avon County Council was convinced that some sort of tram or light rail system was the future. When ATA collapsed, Avon was already moving ahead with plans for a £180m light-rail scheme, to be called the Westway rapid transit project. This never got anywhere.

The rail line between Bristol and Portishead was re-opened too, but for freight, not passengers.

It is now more than 20 years since the Avon Metro scheme failed. The former Avon area has seen some improvements in public transport, such as new generations of buses, dedicated bus lanes and rising numbers of trains on the Severn Beach Line.

Only a masochist, however, would want to spend time looking at the subsequent history of the various attempts to put tram or light rail systems in place. So convoluted and frustrating is the saga of Bristol's (lack of) trams that the best you can say about it is that it's kept council officials in all four of Avon's successor authorities, and, down the years, several consultants, in work.

The one illuminating episode since the demise of the Metro concerned the so-called 'supertram' light rail system. This was probably the best opportunity Bristol had since Advanced Transport for Avon went under. The £200m project was to be a public/private partnership and was given provisional government approval in 2001 as part of a public transport initiative aimed at a number of towns and cities.

It would run from the city centre to Almondsbury using existing rail lines as well as tram lines which would have to be installed. There would be 16 stops, including two former railway stations which would be reopened. This was only to be the first stage; ultimately it was hoped that there would be up to four other routes, all of which would run partly on existing or redundant rail lines.

By this time, Avon had been abolished in favour of four new unitary authorities, and one of the reasons the scheme failed was that Bristol and South Gloucestershire fell out over where the northern terminus should be. Bristol wanted it to stop at a new Park & Ride at Almondsbury, while South Gloucestershire wanted it to run as far as the new shopping centre at Cribbs Causeway.

An independent study showed up various problems with the Cribbs Causeway option, not least an additional £100m on the bill and an extra two years construction time. South Gloucestershire withdrew from the project and Bristol tried to go it alone with a line running to Parkway.

By now, the government was sending out mixed signals over its willingness to fund the project. Faced with a minor financial crisis, Bristol City Council decided to cut its losses. Having spent a lot of money on consultants, studies and indeed the time of its own officials, it effectively killed off the project in June 2004 when it opted to spend £1.5m earmarked for preparatory work on the supertram on keeping down council taxes instead.

The conclusion this led many people to reach was that the Greater Bristol area needed a body with the power to oversee transport planning for the former Avon's four successor councils.

At the time of writing, we have been talking about the need for an 'integrated transport authority' for some years. But then we've been talking about how great it would be to have a tram system for even longer.

Football Grounds 1986-present

Bristol's two professional football teams have rarely been happy with their home grounds, and the last three decades or so have seen both City and Rovers trying to find a new home, or at least improve the existing one.

Of the two, Rovers' tale is the more complicated. It was forced from its traditional home at Eastville stadium (which it did not own) by financial problems in 1986. Pieces of the hallowed turf were sold to fans in pizza boxes, and the club made its temporary home at Bath City FC's Twerton Park ground for ten seasons before returning to Bristol in 1996 to share the Memorial Ground with Bristol Rugby Football Club. Rovers became owners of the 'Mem' a couple of years later.

From the time of the Club's exile to Bath, a prestigious new ground was eagerly desired by directors and fans alike. By the mid-1990s Rovers were hoping to build a stadium on Severnside. Supporters even tried to bring pressure to bear on Bristol City Council to help them out financially by standing candidates in Labour-held wards in the 1994 local elections. This was completely unsuccessful.

Rovers supporters used to joke that Bristol City Council was so called because it was biased towards Bristol City FC, perhaps because so much of the area south of the river was the traditional political stronghold of the (then) controlling Labour group. In the late 1990s Rovers made inquiries into the possibility of building a stadium at Hengrove Park, but were turned down, while a similar approach from City some months later was met with more support from the Council, though this, too, came to nothing.

Of the two teams, City has the more successful record and by the turn of the Millennium was looking for a new ground more in keeping with its ambitions to return to the top levels of English league football. Redevelopment and expansion of its ground at Ashton Gate also remained a possibility, although traffic and parking problems around the stadium were bad enough, and would have become far worse if it were a larger venue attracting Premiership-size crowds.

Despite what Bristol City fans might claim about the proposed Ashton Vale stadium, the greatest might-have-been of Bristol's footballing history came some years before that. This was to have been a new 30,000-seat ground between Pilning and Easter Compton. This new 'Wembley of the West' on Severnside would have been shared by both teams.

It was to have been part of a wider scheme courtesy of Redrow Homes, who, armed with planning permission for industrial development on the 550-acre site, actually wanted to build 1,600 houses instead. This made good commercial sense as the site had excellent motorway access and few conservation issues.

There were problems, of course, such as gaining permission to change the site's use from industry to housing and leisure. The Environment Agency had major concerns about flooding and the Highways Agency would need to be convinced that a new motorway junction would be needed.

While both football clubs signed up to the plan, a lot of fans were sceptical about any possibility that they might have to suspend their traditional animosities. As one fan told a local magazine at the time:

> Saturday afternoon, you meet up with your mates in a nice pub somewhere, have a drink and a chat and then go and endure two hours of misery [he was a Rovers supporter]. With this stadium all you'd get is the two hours of misery.

Satirising the plans, local humour website thatbebristle commented that the stadium proposal also includes 'a major housing development, hotels, conference facilities and its very own year-round traffic jam.'

The project collapsed in 2004 when South Gloucestershire Council made it clear that it would oppose the plan. The scheme's backers, Redrow Homes and South

Gloucestershire Arenas – a consortium of the two soccer clubs and Gaming International – abandoned their intentions of submitting a planning application.

Both clubs now went their separate ways. Rovers would proceed with plans for a brand new stadium on the Memorial Ground site. While it won planning permission for its new ground in 2007, the project was beset by delays, and proved unpopular with many people living in the stadium's neighbourhood. In 2011 the club said it would be moving to a new stadium at the University of the West of England's Frenchay campus and the Memorial ground would be sold to Sainsburys for a new supermarket. Planning permission for the UWE venue was granted in 2012, but progress would then depend on the supermarket plans, which were essential to pay for the new ground.

Meanwhile, in November 2007 Bristol City unveiled plans for a new stadium to be built at Ashton Vale. Its Ashton Gate stadium would be sold to help pay for the development. The fans were enthusiastic about the new 30,000-capacity venue, and HOK, the practice which designed the new Wembley Stadium and Arsenal's Emirates Stadium, was hired to design it.

Of all the developments proposed in Bristol in the last ten years, none has been as controversial, or aroused such passions, as Ashton Vale.

City said it was essential to sell Ashton Gate in order to finance the new stadium, and the most likely buyer would be a supermarket chain. At one point this was going to be Tesco, and then it was to be Sainsbury's. This provoked strong opposition from those who believed that Bristol already has too many large supermarkets, and from some traders, particularly in Bedminster, who feared loss of business.

Opposition also came from residents living near the Ashton Vale site.

In 2009 the project was given added impetus when the F.A. announced that should England win its bid to hold the 2018 World Cup, Bristol would be one of the host cities – assuming the new stadium was ready. The possibility of World Cup football coming to Bristol was very exciting for many.

In 2010, however, an independent inspector recommended that the entire 42-acre Ashton Vale site should be registered as a town green, which would have effectively ruled out any new development. Although planning permission for the stadium was granted by both Bristol and North Somerset councils the following year, the project remained mired in legal disputes over the status of the land. A compromise whereby half of it is town green, while the stadium is built on the other half, may or may not be on the cards. As this book went to press, Rovers were looking forward to building a new stadium at Frenchay in partnership with the University of the West of England, while selling the Memorial ground for a supermarket development. Meanwhile, Bristol City published plans for a new stadium at its existing Ashton Gate site. Hopefully both clubs' long quests will end soon.

Avon Weir 1990-1995

The Bristol Development Corporation (BDC) was one of a number of urban development corporations set up in various cities by the Conservative government in the 1980s and 90s. These were essentially

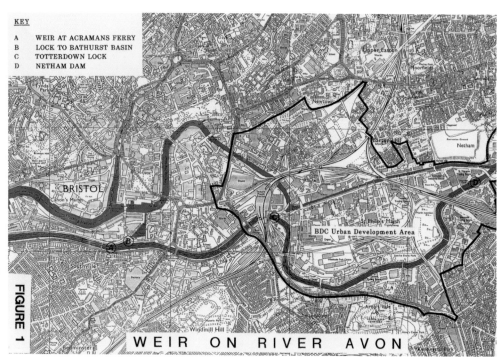

KEY

A   WEIR AT ACRAMANS FERRY
B   LOCK TO BATHURST BASIN
C   TOTTERDOWN LOCK
D   NETHAM DAM

FIGURE 1

WEIR ON RIVER AVON

Map produced for 1990 ▶ feasibility study showing the favoured position of the Avon Weir, plus the 'figure of eight' waterway system it would have created

quangos, and were usually established for a set period, typically five or six years, and their management was largely recruited from the private sector.

With multi-million-pound budgets and their own planning and compulsory purchase powers, they had considerable freedom within the geographical areas assigned to them, and they were expected to regenerate these areas to attract investment and jobs.

The BDC was handed responsibility for a 900-acre stretch of central/east Bristol, including St Philips, The Dings and Crew's Hole. While some of this area included green space on the banks of the Avon, much of it was derelict or semi-derelict former industrial land, particularly around Temple Meads station.

The Corporation had a prickly relationship with

Artist's impression of the weir from Bristol Development Corporation publicity material, 1991 ▼

Bristol City Council. This was partly for ideological reasons; many councillors in the ruling Labour group disliked the idea of this Tory government creation being handed control of a big chunk of the city. There was also a suspicion on the Labour side that the corporation would build a lot of yuppy flats and thus bring more potential Conservative voters into a constituency – Tony Benn had until recently been its MP – which Labour was desperate to win back from the Tories.

There were less overtly political concerns, too. Some feared the BDC would build shops and offices which would drive out the last remaining manufacturing and engineering jobs left in the area. Furthermore, the Council was heavily focussed on redeveloping Bristol's Harbourside area at this time, and councillors and officials feared the BDC would compete for public funding and private sector investment.

By the time the BDC had been wound up in 1995, the area had seen the construction of 670 new houses. According to government figures, 4,825 jobs had been created and £235m of investment had been brought into the area. Despite its lifespan being extended by two years, the BDC had failed to meet most of its initial targets. While some BDC members later blamed the obstructiveness of the Council, its biggest challenge had been a flatlining economy which had discouraged investment.

The BDC's most visible achievements were the Avonmeads retail and leisure park (including the Showcase, Bristol's first multiplex cinema) and the St Philips Causeway 'Spine Road' connecting Bath Road to Lawrence Hill to relieve traffic pressure around Temple Meads. It also laid the groundwork for the Temple Quarter development. If its short-term results were disappointing, the BDC had laid the foundations for much of the Bristol building boom which would soon follow. It might also be argued that it played a significant part in shifting Bristol's centre of gravity eastwards.

The BDC was committed to sorting out the infrastructure of the area as a starting point, and there were two elements to this. The first was the Spine Road, the second was Avon Weir.

Avon Weir would have been an unspectacular structure, built at a comparatively low cost – much less than the £50m spine road. Had it been built, however, it could potentially have had a very dramatic effect across much of Bristol, and could even have altered the city's entire character.

For much of each day, the tidal Avon in Bristol is a small trickle at the bottom of brown, muddy banks. In the 1980s there were many parts of the city – most within the BDC area – where it presented a particularly depressing spectacle, with large amounts of rubbish exposed at low tide. Much of this was against a backdrop of post-industrial dereliction. The Avon Weir was a possible solution to this. It would dam the river, permanently impounding the water at a constant level. This would then provide attractive waterside vistas for the development of homes and workplaces. It would also provide huge potential for recreational activities, such as fishing and boating.

This was exactly the sort of project that the BDC thought it should be involved with, as it would turn a 4km stretch of eyesore – that is, 8km of riverbank on both sides – into sites which would be attractive to investors. The land values would shoot up, and homes, offices, shops and leisure developments

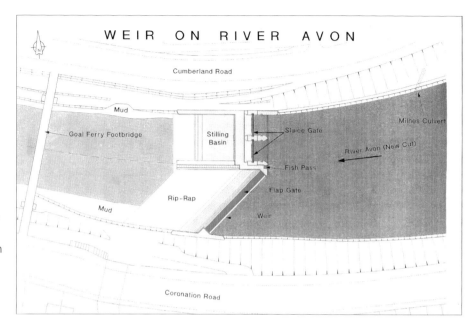

WEIR ON RIVER AVON

Cumberland Road

Mud

Goal Ferry Footbridge

Stilling Basin

Sluice Gate

Milnes Culvert

River Avon (New Cut)

Fish Pass

Mud

Rip-Rap

Flap Gate

Weir

Coronation Road

Weir structure and location from the 1990 feasibility study carried out for the Bristol Development Corporation

would soon follow.

Initially, the favoured location for the barrage would be close to Bath Bridge, near Temple Meads station. A feasibility carried out by WS Atkins in 1990 said it was viable, and so a more detailed study was carried out by Sir Alexander Gibb & Partners later the same year. It looked at seven potential sites for a barrier and shortlisted three – Totterdown Lock, Bath Bridge and Acraman's Ferry. It recommended the latter, which is the stretch of river close to Bathurst Basin and the Gaol Ferry pedestrian bridge.

A barrier here would open up even more development potential. The river could now be raised to the same level as the Floating Harbour and the Feeder Canal, and could be linked to them via Bathurst Basin. This would create an enormous figure-of-eight-shaped waterway. More than half of this, on the eastern side, was within the BDC area, and on its banks was a huge amount of former industrial land in need of redevelopment.

The BDC bullishly predicted that the Weir project would attract around £300m of private investment, and create 8,000 jobs.

The design which Gibb, working with Hydraulics Research Ltd, recommended was for a weir with a floodgate, as it would cost less than a gated barrage, would cost less to maintain, and it would look more interesting. It would be 30 metres long and aligned diagonally to the river flow. Normal flows would pass over the weir but its gates would be opened if upstream flows increased to flood proportions. For tidal salt water surges coming from the other direction there was a sort of flap on top ('adjustable weir crest') which could be raised to exclude all but the

▲ From run-down and depressing former industrial area to pleasant waterside leisure facility, thanks to the Avon Weir. Illustration from an early 1990s Bristol Development Corporation brochure

highest tides.

The Gibb plan estimated the cost of the scheme at £7.96m in 1990 prices. Some £2.7m of this would be related to sewerage works. The document goes on to note, however, that it would have had a number of knock-on consequences for the wider city's drainage and flood defences, some of which should be paid for by other agencies, such as Wessex Water or Bristol City Council.

To build the Weir would have required further powers that the BDC did not have, and an Act of Parliament received royal assent in March 1992. By this time BDC reckoned the project would cost £10m.

The plan simply faded away in the face of harsh economic times. The money which would have funded the Weir was to have come from capital receipts from the massive development that the BDC planned around Temple Meads station, but this simply wasn't forthcoming.

The BDC focussed on its other major infrastruc-

ture project, the Spine Road, which did eventually get built. Unlike the Spine Road, the Avon Weir plan did not encounter much political opposition, and though there were definite concerns about its effect on wildlife, the Avon Weir project was quietly shelved because it had no quick wins.

By the time the BDC was wound up in 1995, the city was already embarking on a building boom, with new office and housing developments springing up everywhere, with waterside sites commanding most of the biggest investment.

The Avon Weir would almost certainly have boosted demand for waterside homes and offices even further. It would probably also have speeded up a number of developments, such as around the Courage Brewery near Bristol Bridge, or the old Bristol General Hospital site. Its effect on the wider image of Bristol can only be guessed at, though by opening up huge stretches of waterways to development and leisure, one can easily imagine advertising and marketing campaigns aimed at tourists and relocating businesses selling Bristol as 'England's Venice' for all they're worth.

Harbourside Centre 1996-1998

The Harbourside Centre project had its public launch at an elaborate photocall in September 1997. Lord Gowrie, Chairman of the Arts Council of England, arrived at the Lloyds Amphitheatre by helicopter bearing a cheque for £4.3m. Also present were prominent members of the Council and the local business community. There were leading figures from

Model of the Behnisch design for the Harbourside Centre. If this was 2012, Bordeaux Quay would be to the right, while over in the distance on the left is M-Shed ▶

The Behnisch design. (Both images: Christian Kandzia/Behnisch Architekten) ▶

the arts, too, including members of Massive Attack. At this time, the band, and the 'Bristol Sound' in general, were nearing the peak of their global reach.

The Harbourside Centre, also known locally as the Centre for the Performing Arts, was a focal point in the regeneration of the Canon's Marsh area. The landmark concert hall and performance venue, with its striking design, would be Bristol's answer to the Sydney Opera House.

As he handed over the cheque, which would enable the next stages of the project to succeed, Lord Gowrie famously compared it to an exploding greenhouse.

The project had been put out to an international design competition in 1996. It was won by Behnisch & Behnisch of Stuttgart. The firm explained the thinking behind its vision:

> The unique, sculptural figure of the proposed building not only describes an easily identifiable image for the Harbourside Centre, but also, through contrast, heightens the qualities of the neighbouring Harbourside buildings. The complexity of the exterior form allows the building to present different scales when viewed from across the harbour, from street level or from the hills above the city.

Due to be completed by 2002, the building would accommodate a 2,300-capacity concert venue, plus a smaller 450-seat auditorium.

It would also be the product of a powerful coalition of the Council, the private sector and the local arts community. Everyone in official Bristol was behind it.

Harbourside Director Duncan Fraser unveiled a

▲ The concert hall and performance venue, with its striking design, would be Bristol's answer to the Sydney Opera House. (Christian Kandzia/Behnisch Architekten)

series of musical residencies for the centre including the Bournemouth Symphony Orchestra and the Orchestra for the Age of Enlightenment. The Centre would even have its own composer-in-residence and in-house choreographer, Lea Anderson, whose dance companies the Cholmondeleys and the Featherstone-haughs would also take residence. South West Arts Chairman Graham Long then spoke of the Harbourside not just as a centre for the arts in Bristol but a focus for arts and music throughout the region.

Speeches safely over, a celebration party kicked off at the nearby Leadworks. While a live band played improvised jazz, canapés and champagne were passed around by dancers disguised as waitresses. The only hiccup came when 3D and Mushroom from Massive Attack – to the dismay of the assembled PR people – told local TV crews that the centre was too small, too elitist and would not be suitable for live performances from Bristol's most successful musicians.

The total cost of the Harbourside Centre was projected at £89m. Some would be raised in sponsorship, some would come from Bristol City Council, which was also pledged to provide over £1m a year in revenue funding during the Centre's early years.

The bulk of the money, however, some £58m, would come from the Arts Council's Lottery Capital Programme. While obviously the project would have to go through a lengthy and rigorous application process for the money, it was widely understood that the bid was looked on with favour. The fact that the Arts Council gave almost £5m to help get the project started showed that it wanted the bid to succeed.

In March 1998 Jeremy Newton, the Arts Council's National Lottery Director, wrote to Louis Sherwood, Chairman of the Harbourside Centre project, confirming his support. 'The sum of £58 million,' he wrote,

> represents a reasonable planning figure on which to base your funding assumptions. Naturally I cannot at this stage, in the absence of a full application, confirm an absolute commitment of this

sum. Nevertheless, subject to satisfaction of the Lottery Funding criteria, the project represents a confirmed element of the Arts Council's capital strategy and I have no doubt that we will, in due course, be able to play our full part in ensuring the success of the project.

Shortly afterwards, however, things began to look less promising, particularly when the Arts Council sent in a team of assessors to examine the project in minute detail. Councillor Paul Smith, chair of Bristol's Leisure Services Committee and a member of the Harbourside Centre board later said: 'They were sent in to find things wrong with the project. They were very aggressive. They were a hit squad, basically.'

On Thursday July 30 1998, the Arts Council issued a terse statement saying the application for the £58m had been rejected. 'Contrary to Arts Council advice,' it said, 'the Harbourside project has not applied adequate dedicated senior level executive expertise to ensure the necessary leadership and direction for a project of this magnitude.'

In its statement about its decision to reject the Harbourside Centre bid, the Arts Council listed a number of 'flaws' with the proposal. The design brief and cost information was incomplete, the business plan was not thought through properly, there wasn't enough involvement on the part of other cultural organisations in the region.

The Arts Council's points were vague, and all firmly rebutted in detail by the Harbourside Centre board. The ensuing row was understandably bitter. The Harbourside Centre board accused the Arts Council of moving the goalposts. Certainly the idea that somehow they were lacking 'senior level executive expertise' was curious given that the board included the chief executive of Bristol & West, the chair of Wessex Water and a former leader of Bristol City Council. Harbourside Centre Chairman Louis Sherwood (former Chairman of a supermarket chain, and at this time chairman of HTV West) said:

> The new chairman and chief executive of the Arts Council are implementing a new policy and were casting around for reasons to reject a £58m application. We have been stitched up.

Tony Blair's new Labour government, elected the previous year, changed the way in which Lottery money was distributed, adding a new 'good cause' – health, education and the environment – thus cutting the Arts Council's share of the Lottery pot.

Then Lord Gowrie, a former Conservative Arts Minister, was succeeded as chair of the Arts Council by Gerry Robinson, a businessman handpicked by Tony Blair. Robinson implemented a wholesale overhaul of the Arts Council board and ushered in a new regime in which less money was to be spent on big capital projects, and more would in smaller packages to community groups, or as revenue funding for venues and artists.

As one board member told *Venue* magazine afterwards: 'They killed it because it was expensive . . . Basically the project would have taken nearly a quarter of their money for the next five years. They couldn't say they didn't have enough money because that'd leave them with egg on their faces, so they decided to attack the management of the Centre instead.'

Some £5m of public and private money was spent on the project; aside from £1m which was the Centre's share of the cost of the Harbourside underground car park, all of it was now lost.

Fifteen years on, Behnisch & Behnisch were still displaying the plans and models for the centre on its website, proud of the radical design. At the time of writing, the site, between the Lloyds TSB building and Bordeaux Quay, is still vacant.

The People's Cultural Palace

1997‒

'Let's make Bristol the Jerusalem of England,' said businessman Ravi Pandya, proposing that the city should have a massive building for citizens of all faiths and cultures. 'We are nearing the end of the millennium, and there is so much hatred and conflict in the world. I thought it would be good to do something useful, to create a place for reconciliation amongst all the people of the world. I thought we could build a palace in Bristol. On the waterfront.'

Of all the major structures that might have been built in Bristol in the last 50 years, the People's Cultural Palace is the most idealistic. It had no real funding base, but was to be built on donations of time and money from across the city. But for a while at least the plan attracted a fair amount of support.

Pandya, a Hindu, arrived from Kenya in 1971 and was married to a Roman Catholic. His vision for the Palace, he said, came to him while attending a Christmas service at the Anglican St Mary Redcliffe.

Sketch of a possible design ▶ for the People's Cultural Palace. (David Innes Wilkin, Chartered Architect RIBA)

The Cultural Palace would be a place where children and adults from all races and creeds could learn about one another, not just through religion, but through art, music, theatre, craftwork, food and more. It would be built in a rainbow mixture of architectural styles reflecting Bristol's different faiths and cultures. Brick, marble, jade, Bath stone, concrete ... Everything would go into the mix.

Writing in the *Evening Post* in July 1997, he said:

Our skyline would have spice and flavour. Curry has become a national dish of Britain; Spice Girls are adding a bit of flavour to the national scene ... So certainly, a beautiful building reflecting Gothic, Flemish, Moghul, Hindu and other architecture would add spice to our skyline!

Some formal plans and costings were drawn up, and some outline sketches of what it might look like were prepared on a voluntary basis by Bristol architect David Innes Wilkin. It would comprise three sections, perhaps with three domes, dedicated to creativity, religion and discussion. The first was to be for the arts and crafts, and a venue for functions, festivals and performances which would also contain restaurants and shops selling crafts from around the world. The Dome of Faiths would be a place of meditation and prayer and would host preachers of all faiths as well as events to educate children and adults about the world's religions. There would also be permanent or temporary exhibitions on such issues as the environment and sustainability, and the movement for the abolition of slavery. At this time Bristol still had its Exploratory hands-on science centre (soon to be replaced by Explore-At-Bristol) and Pandya said that the Dome of Faiths would be 'a spiritual exploratory'. The third, the Dome of Peace, would have an exhibition space and conference centre.

Pandya gathered a dedicated team of supporters from across the city's different communities, and launched an appeal for volunteers and money. If every one of 500,000 or so people living in Bristol and its immediate outskirts donated just 50p a week, there would be more than enough money to build the temple within three years. Fifty pence was less than the sum the average Bristolian was spending on the Lottery each week, he pointed out. If the project did not succeed, monies raised would go to the RSPCA and homeless charities.

The costs were estimated at anything between £20m and £60m. The committee were inspired by the example of the Hindu Neasden Temple in north London, much of which had been built by local volunteer work and donations, but which had also, for example, employed craftsmen in India to carve marble which had been shipped from Europe and when completed, was sent to Neasden for incorporation into the building.

Various locations were proposed; there was a possible site close to the Industrial Museum (now M Shed). On another occasion, the Council suggested a site at Oldbury Court, though the Palace Committee preferred a central location, preferably somewhere on or near the Harbour.

While the local establishment paid polite lip-service to the idea, there was plenty of private scepticism. One local grandee allegedly asked Mr Pandya: 'Would you be doing yogic flying and squatting on the floor?'

There was also some misunderstanding, with its being referred to as a 'mosque' and a 'Bombay Palace'. This was despite Pandya's adamant repetition that it was for people of all faiths and none, and that one of its day-to-day functions would be as a wedding venue from which no religion would be excluded.

At this time, official Bristol was focussed on the redevelopment of Harbourside, particularly the Harbourside Centre and the At-Bristol attractions. There may even have been fears that these and other projects might lose funding if the Palace were to go ahead.

Ultimately, with neither enough money, nor a definite site, the project fizzled out, particularly once key members of the committee died. Pandya and the Cultural Palace organisation did, however, remain active for many years, promoting interfaith events and trying to foster understanding between communities.

The Orbit Millennium Project
1996-1997

This was to be a vast scale-model of the solar system which would cover the whole of Bristol. Launching the bid to gain support, sponsors and funding, the organisers said:

Few realise the immense distances that lie between the planets and how relatively small they are. One of the objects of the Orbit Millennium Project is to convey some sense of this by positioning a giant true-to-scale solar system in

Artist's impression of the Sun orrery which would have been in Millennium Square. (Inscape Architects) ▶

Bristol as it is configured at the dawn of the Millennium. The sun and inner planets will lie in the docks, close to the Lloyds building and in the proposed New World Square. Jupiter and Saturn are in Bedminster, Uranus close to the Plimsoll Bridge, Neptune in Ashton Court Park and the outermost planet, Pluto, in the Downs.

The Orbit Millennium Project was conceived by Martin Rieser, a senior lecturer in electronic media at the Faculty of Art, Media and Design at the University of the West of England, and by Mike Richards, a founding partner at a leading Bristol architectural practice, Inscape.

The proposal quickly captured the imagination and enthusiasm of Bristolians. Once they understood the concept, everyone was fascinated and bemused by the scales involved. The Sun, positioned in what would later be known as Millennium Square but which at the time was to be called New World Square, would be 840mm in diameter. Earth would be 100 yards from the sun and about the size of a pea. Jupiter, the largest planet, would be the size of a grapefruit. Pluto would be a mile and a half away on the Downs to the north of the Suspension Bridge, and would measure less than a fifth of a centimetre.

Each planet would be positioned to correspond to where they would rise on the first day of the year 2000.

Because so many of the planets were so tiny, each would be housed within a 'window' inside a three-sided obelisk six metres high. The nine obelisks would be finished in fine materials, such as granite, marble, glass, bronze and stainless steel, the colour and texture of each chosen to match the characteristics of each planet. Each would be designed by an artist to reflect the place of each planet in mythology, and would feature inscribed scientific information on the planet in question.

Meanwhile, at the centre of the scheme the sun would be covered by a glass dome which would also contain an orrery – an interactive moving display of the solar system. There were also to be sensors so that as people moved around it, they would break beams to create music patterns. This 'Music of the Spheres' was to be composed and programmed by veteran Bristol composer Edward Williams, well-known for his work on interactive music.

The project was a perfect fit with the planned interactive science centre which would later open as Explore-At-Bristol. There were also plans to create walking/running trails around Bristol's own solar system. Local enthusiasm was so strong that one councillor complained that there wasn't going to be a planet in his ward.

Both the sun dome and the obelisks were also to be topped with lasers which would project beams into the night sky on special occasions, of which the start of the new millennium would certainly have been one. At a public launch of the project in July 1996 a prototype obelisk, made and donated by local firm City Engineering, was displayed, complete with laser.

While it could probably have been completed successfully for less than £1.5m, the Millennium Commission rejected the project's funding application. The organisers believe that the most likely reason for this was the ten lasers; each would have cost around £60,000, and there would have been high maintenance costs as well.

The Orbit Millennium Project remains one of the most intriguing Bristol might-have-beens from recent years. Its costs would have been small (especially if the lasers were omitted), it would have taken up very

▲ The prototype obelisk on display at the project launch in 1996. (Inscape Architects)

little space and it would have had real artistic and educational value. You can easily see how it would have become one of the things that visitors to Bristol were told they simply have to see.

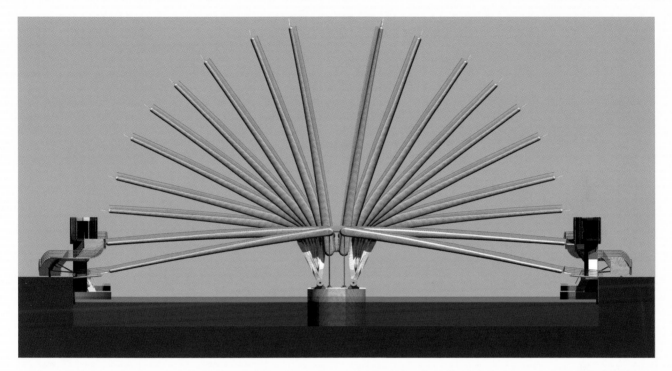

WINGBRIDGE

One of the most intriguing ideas to be generated by the redevelopment of Harbourside was the 'Wingbridge', a pedestrian bridge which would have linked Gas Ferry Road on Spike Island (next to the ss *Great Britain*) to Gas Ferry Road in Canon's Marsh.

Many debates have raged about the redevelopment of the City Docks down the years, and the Wingbridge addressed two of them. The first was over the way in which the lion's share of investment, building and jobs has gone to the northern side. There was a widespread feeling south of the river that the area was missing out, so a bridge would have been a way of connecting the south to the booming north.

The other issue is over whether or not the Floating Harbour should have any more bridges at all. Many people felt – still feel – that uninterrupted water looks best, and that bridges make life harder for boats and ships. Certainly a low bridge in this location would have made it impossible for tall ships to come in for the Harbour Festival. The Wingbridge was an elegant solution; its decks could rise into the air, like a giant pair of butterfly wings, to allow shipping through.

It was devised by Bristol firms Barlow Henley Architects and engineers Fenton Holloway in 2003. Although no finance or funding had been secured, the firms submitted a planning application to sound out public and official views. With little official support, it remains on the drawing-board.

(Picture: Barlow Henley Architects)

Bristol Venice/Little Venice

1999–2001

After the old City Docks were saved from being filled in/covered over in the 1970s, everyone was in broad agreement that the area should be regenerated with housing, cultural and entertainment venues, pubs, restaurants, commercial sites and water-based leisure facilities. But within the detail, there were still plenty of controversies.

One of the most difficult areas to redevelop was around Canon's Marsh, where there were a number of separate landowners, and a long history of industrial and transport usage. The initial log jam was broken when the Council agreed to Lloyds Bank's plans to build an office complex there. One of the reasons the Labour Council gave Lloyds the go-ahead was that this part of the Docks might have been handed over to the Bristol Development Corporation, and the Council was keen to retain control of the area.

A Harbourside Sponsors Group was formed in 1992, bringing together landowners, Council, business, and other stakeholders and Millennium Square, Wildscreen World (later Wildwalk) and more would materialise, while other projects, such as the Harbourside Centre (see earlier) did not.

One of the biggest controversies, however, was over land to the west of Millennium Square. This was mostly privately owned and was to be redeveloped by Crest Nicholson. Wanting to maximise their returns, the firm put forward a mixed-use scheme including a large leisure centre and multiplex cinema which was immediately condemned as too big for the setting,

▲ Model of the Little Venice/Bristol Venice proposal. (Ferguson Mann Architects)

particularly as it would dominate the Cathedral, or obscure views of it.

Crest Nicholson then put forward a revised plan in which the buildings were smaller but which still ran into furious opposition. The Planning Committee meeting at the Council House in January 2000 was very well-attended, with most people speaking against the proposal. Paul Chadd QC, veteran of so many planning rows before now, was only one of many articulate critics of the proposals when he urged the Council to reject 'this low and pathetic abortion of a scheme.'

The joker in the pack was local architect George Ferguson, who had also taken an active role in many of the 1960s and '70s campaigns against various big developments. He did not have the support of the landowners – Crest Nicholson had been appointed the developers – but he nonetheless put forward an alternative scheme which became known as 'Little Venice' but which he calls 'Bristol Venice.'

Bristol Venice would have done away with the leisure centre and built on lower levels. At its centre would have been a canal, thus actually increasing the amount of waterside property. It would also have kept the last dockside cargo transit shed in the vicinity. The latter building was destroyed in a fire shortly afterwards.

Ferguson said later:

To build big view-blocking buildings would have been very damaging. We set up a structure built around views of the cathedral, and learning from old places that we enjoy. We'd lost the whole concept of street and square; old cities retain their original medieval pattern usually, so you're usually rebuilding along that structure. The idea was to make something on a human scale that could be renewed again and again over time.

Ferguson Mann Architects were backed by an anonymous local developer, though, says Ferguson, neither he nor they believed there was any realistic prospect of the scheme being adopted. It was, rather, he says, 'an alternative view to show people there was a better way.'

Bristol Venice was given planning permission by the Council in 2001, but the owners of the site – British Gas, Lloyds TSB, British Rail (as was) and Bristol City Council – were sticking with Crest Nicholson. Further revised plans were finally accepted in full in 2004.

The Bristol Pyramid (now The Pyramid) 1999-present

In the run-up to the Millennium, Frank Drake, artist-in-residence at the CREATE Centre, came up with an idea which generated a huge amount of media interest and public enthusiasm.

He proposed building a huge pyramid, made from over 300,000 wine bottles. This would be erected on top of the B Bond building (which houses the CREATE Centre and the Bristol Record Office) and, since it was originally conceived as a project to mark the Millennium, it would stay up there for a year. The idea was to represent the CREATE Centre's ethos of Sustainability and Recycling, and to celebrate the Millennium.

It was claimed that this 400-tonne structure would be the largest ever artwork (up to that time, anyway) made from recycled materials. It would comprise 1,024 triangular 'tiles', each of 300 bottles, and would be lit from the inside using solar-generated electricity to provide a glowing green landmark at night.

The project would also have a website corresponding to the actual triangular frames (tiles) which would represent communities within towns and cities of every country in the world and the bottles would represent the messages of individuals within these cities and towns. The real bottles would also contain letters from local schoolchildren. It would also have some of the newfangled webcams on top, providing visitors to the website with views over Bristol.

Consultant engineers addressed any concerns about putting such a massive structure on top of B Bond,

▲ Artist's impression of the Pyramid on top of the CREATE centre, lit from the inside at night using solar-generated electricity. (Pyramid Foundation)

a former tobacco bonded warehouse. Planning permission was secured, the Bristol Pyramid Foundation was granted charitable status and Drake and his team set about raising the money, none of which was to come from public funds. Bath-based musician Peter Gabriel proved an enthusiastic backer, and sponsored the first tile.

In late 2000 the Foundation began collecting 'Dream Day' messages from local primary school-children to put in the bottles. These messages were going to be available on the website, as well as being recorded on a CD-ROM which would be placed at the top of the Pyramid. The messages in bottles were, however, to take second-place to the Pyramid's most important educational function locally, which was to 'use humour, creativity and innovation to demonstrate mathematics and geometry' as well as the importance of recycling and sustainability.

▲ Early Pyramid supporter, musician Peter Gabriel with one of the tiles. (Pyramid Foundation)

By the autumn of 2001 the original scheme was abandoned. Bristol City Council, which owns B Bond, claimed that the Pyramid Foundation's business plan failed 'to address serious concerns relating to the financial and structural viability of the project.' It was not convinced the project could raise the estimated £2.5m cost.

The Bristol Pyramid Foundation disagreed strongly. In a press statement it said,

> It is the firm belief of Frank Drake and the trustees of the Bristol Pyramid Foundation that the business plan submitted to Bristol City Council gave more than enough detail for a project at its current stage of development. Especially as the Council was not being asked to contribute to the construction costs and ... no construction work would be undertaken until all necessary monies for construction and eventual dis-assembly had been found.

The Pyramid Foundation, however, is still going. 'The Cell' which is 1/64th of one side of the Pyramid, was on display at the University of the West of England's Bower Ashton site until 2012, with further plans to display it elsewhere. The Foundation still hopes to build the Pyramid in its entirety.

According to Frank Drake:

> The Pyramid Foundation will find a site elsewhere and The Pyramid will be constructed (the world is our oyster!) with a council that appreciates and recognises the importance of recycling and sustainability.

Bristol Arena 2003-2007

Bristol lacks a performance venue for major touring bands. The Colston Hall can accommodate around 2,000 people, but the biggest acts pass Bristol by. To see really big-name international musicians, Bristol's music fans have to travel to Cardiff, London or Birmingham.

One of the greatest ironies in this is that in the 1980s and 90s Bristol produced a succession of artists of global stature. Acts coming from Bristol, or closely associated with the city, included PJ Harvey, Massive Attack, Roni Size/Reprazent, Portishead and many others. Yet when Massive Attack performed in their home town for the first time in some years in December 1998, they played four successive nights at Bristol University Union's Anson Rooms – though this was also because of their refusal to play the Colston Hall on account of its association with a slave trader.

For a comparatively small city, Bristol punches well above its weight culturally, and yet it does not have a performance venue to match.

The problem with big venues is that they are expensive to build and maintain. The best-run ones might be packed with sell-out crowds several nights a month, but for most of the time there's just a very large building which is empty.

By the early 2000s, though, it was starting to look as though Bristol might indeed get the venue it wanted. The South West Regional Development Agency (SWRDA), the quango charged with boosting the region's economy, had joined forces with Bristol City Council to look into the issue.

Any venue attracting several thousand people from around the region would need good transport links, but the Council was adamant from the outset that it would never support a development on the edge of the city. If it was going to invest public money in this project, it had to be for something which would bring people (and their spending power) into the middle of the city.

Several sites were looked at, but the one chosen was a former diesel locomotive yard right next to Temple Meads station. SWRDA acquired the nine-acre plot which was part of the wider Temple Quay regeneration project.

From the viewpoint of SWRDA and the Council, building the Arena, as it was now being called, was worth a try. The plan was for the two public bodies to acquire the site, clear it, put the road and utility infrastructures in place and give planning permission. A private firm would build and run the arena. Even if the project failed, the taxpayer would not lose out too much because the land would be of great value to any developer wanting to build flats or offices.

Work started on clearing the site in late 2003, and a private partner was chosen two years later. This was Bristol Waterside Arena Ltd (BWA), a consortium including SMG, a US-based firm which operates sports stadiums and entertainment venues worldwide. The team also included Orion Land & Leisure, Sir Robert McAlpine and Bellway. The group would build and operate the arena, and would develop the rest of the site as well.

Planning applications were submitted, a public consultation was held and work started on detailed designs for a venue with a capacity of between 10,000 and 12,000. To make it stack up financially, it would also have conference and exhibition facilities, and there was confident talk of its staging sporting events as well as music.

Many residents in the area were concerned. People living in Totterdown, for instance, were naturally fearful that concert-goers would not all arrive by train, and that their streets would be clogged up by crazed heavy metal fans looking for free parking spaces.

Nonetheless, work continued. In March 2006 BWA announced it had chosen its architects. Burland TM would be masterplanner of the entire development, reckoned to cost £150m in total, while HOK Sport Architecture would design the arena itself. The Arena

▲ An early publicity handout: artist's impression of what the Bristol Arena might have looked like

was set to open by December 2008.

The full story of why and how the project failed has yet to come out, but the fundamental problems were twofold. First, how do you create and run a major attraction in the middle of a busy area where the roads are already overstretched? Secondly, how do you make it a commercial proposition?

While SWRDA and the Council were spending millions on the site, and had earmarked many millions more to help make the arena happen, it would never be possible to build it without the private sector. The deal with the developers was that they would be paid in land; they could build offices, apartments, shops and other leisure facilities around the arena site. The profit developers made from building on these additional landholdings would, in theory, enable the Arena to be built and run without the necessity for any public subsidy.

MUSEUM OF BRISTOL

A museum telling the story of Bristol and its people had long been a local ambition, and work finally started in the early 2000s. The site would be a former dockside transit shed built in the 1950s, and by then home to Bristol's Industrial Museum. It finally opened in 2011 following a troubled gestation dogged by cost overruns.

An earlier controversy centred on the original design by LAB Architecture Studios unveiled in 2005. This would have stripped the building back to its steel frame and created a new glass-fronted structure (pictured). Many locals objected to the design, seeing it as a needless destruction of the harbour's heritage. A campaign group was formed, meetings were held, and the following year the Council asked the architects to come up with a new design which preserved the building's historic frontage.

(Picture: LAB Architecture Studio)

This was never going to be a simple commercial development. Because of the involvement both of SWRDA and the Council, any expenditure of public money, or disposal of assets (land), was covered by a wide range of regulations.

Behind closed doors, the developers, SWRDA and the Council argued over what, exactly, could be built around the site. From the viewpoint of developers in the boom years of the early twenty-first century, the most profitable thing you could build was usually flats. They wanted to build a lot of apartments, while the Council, already worried about the traffic implications of the arena, wanted to limit the amount of new residents and their cars.

The soil on the site had been impregnated over several decades with diesel, and in November 2007 SWRDA announced that work had started on the £4.2m programme to decontaminate the site. The following month it was announced that the Arena project had collapsed. It had simply not been possible to strike a balance between the wishes of all the different parties.

The announcement triggered a great deal of anger locally, both in the press and on internet forums. People started petitions demanding that the project be re-started. Predictably enough it was SWRDA, unpopular, unelected and with a reputation for spending taxpayers' money rather too freely, which took nearly all the flak.

Shortly after being elected mayor at the end of 2012, George Ferguson pledged that an arena would be built on the Temple Meads site.

The St Paul's Tower 2006-2012

In 2007 developers PG Enterprises and housing firm Places for People (PfP) announced that they were looking into the possibility of building the South West's tallest skyscraper in St Paul's, close to the M32.

The 40-storey tower would have been more than twice the height of Bristol's tallest structures, the spire of St Mary Redcliffe (292ft) and the Castlemead office block (262ft). It would also be taller than some of the City of London's most iconic modern buildings such as the Swiss Re building or the 'Gherkin'.

The skyscraper was one of a set of options put forward for the regeneration of a site in Dove Lane. Each of the options included a mix of houses and flats as well as community facilities, offices, shops and work spaces.

One of the advantages put forward for a skyscraper was that it would free up space on the rest of the site for open spaces and possibly a market. Dr Colin Bloch, a director of PG Enterprises, told the *Evening Post*:

Although it would be the tallest building in Bristol, we would also hope it would be the most sustainable and architecturally exciting feature of this gateway site to a prospering city.

Developers and owners said that they hoped to generate around 1,000 much-needed jobs and create a thriving community, and the project could be completed by 2010.

As a not-for-dividend enterprise which took its responsibilities to the community seriously, PfP

▲ One of the Dove Lane redevelopment options offered to local residents. This was the second skyscraper proposal, shorter than the original 600ft proposal. (Places for People)

emphasised that the skyscraper was just one option for the site and would not be built if locals did not support it.

This support was not wholehearted. A representative of community group St Pauls Unlimited told the press:

> I think it is wishful thinking on the part of the developer ... I think people in St Paul's will not want something which totally dominates the area and looks completely out of place.

Plans were complicated later in 2007 when the Council offered the developers an adjacent former school site as well. A second set of options was presented to the community, one of which included a tower, although this time round it would only have been 28 storeys high.

No planning application for a skyscraper was ever submitted. In early 2012 Bristol City Council approved a regeneration plan for the 4.5 acre site put forward by Places for People which included homes, business start-up and social enterprise facilities, shops, a health centre and improved public space. The plans followed extensive consultation and design workshops with the local community.

The Chocolate Factory and Cycle Houses 2006-2010

The last chocolates rolled off the production line at the Elizabeth Shaw factory in Greenbank at the end of 2006.

A big site like this in an increasingly popular residential area was bound to attract the attention of property developers, and Persimmon Homes rapidly pounced with plans to demolish the Victorian building and build 100 or so houses. Local residents and conservationists were outraged and a planning inspector ruled against the scheme.

The site was sold to another property developer, Bristol firm Squarepeg, for a reported £5m. The company pledged to keep the buildings and redevelop them, and it consulted with residents in the neighbourhood about its plans for the site.

In 2008 Squarepeg submitted a planning application to Bristol City Council for 186 houses and flats on the former factory site, plus a further 66 new-build homes on the land around it. There would also be cafés, community spaces and some office/business space as well, plus some mini-allotments.

The Chocolate Factory had one big attention-grabbing feature – 22 'cycle houses'. The site is right next to the Bristol & Bath Railway cycle path and to architect George Ferguson it made good sense to make some of the accommodation bike-friendly. The cycle houses – 12 of which would be right next to the path – were said at the time to be the first such

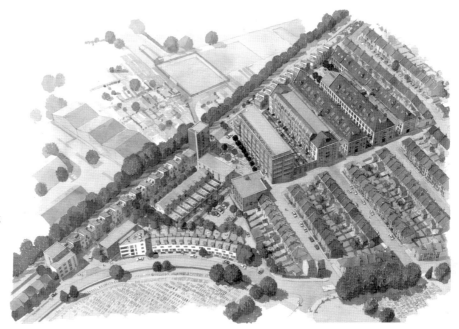

Artist's impression of the Greenbank chocolate factory development. (Ferguson Mann Architects) ▶

◀
Impression of the cycle houses next to the Bristol & Bath Railway Path. (Ferguson Mann Architects)

homes of their kind in Britain. Ferguson saw a chance here to repeat the success he had had with the Tobacco Factory in Southville by re-using former industrial buildings which had once been at the heart of the community.

However, part of the plan required the Council to sell the developer a strip of land alongside the site for four of the cycle homes and for a seven storey 'Cycle Dock' building. This was envisaged as a cycle garage/repair centre for residents, and possibly even act as a hostel where cyclists making long journeys could stay overnight.

This ran into immediate controversy, with some local residents, cycling campaigners and environmentalists saying that the sale of the strip of green land was unnecessary, and that the development would have a negative impact on the cycle path. Squarepeg insisted that the entire development would be one of the greenest and most sustainable the city had ever seen.

Planning permission was granted the following year, but this was subject to a so-called 'Section 106' agreement being finalised. This is where a developer makes some contribution to the wider community as a result of 'planning gain' – the increase in a site's value when planning permission has been secured. Squarepeg was originally supposed to make £1.5m worth of contributions towards local education, roads and open spaces, but as the economy declined, this was cut back to £90,000.

As business confidence declined further, the developers realised that they would have difficulties raising the finance, and the land had dropped dramatically in value. At the time of writing the site remains derelict, although it will almost certainly be redeveloped.

A Transatlantic Tunnel, Hurrah!

You can separate most – but not all – of the projects in this book into two broad categories; those that should never be built, and those which one day will be built.

We may not get a full-blown Severn Barrage, but someone will be generating electricity from the Severn's tides sooner or later. Bristol will probably one day have some sort of performance arena, plus a sports stadium or two. The Avon may well be 'dockised', just not in the way the Victorians imagined, nor for the reasons that they had.

As for the big unbuilt projects of the future, we know for certain what one of them will be.

Houses.

Plenty of homes will be built, but plenty of other housing schemes will be blocked.

There are never enough houses, and there never have been. That is, there have never been enough affordable ones.

In almost all the history of almost every city in the world, the shortage of decent housing at reasonable prices/rents is a constant. Bristol is no different. It's rarely been a question of whether there's a shortage, but of how bad it is. Probably the only time that Bristolians felt there was enough accommodation for all would have been shortly after the Black Death.

The rest of Bristol's history contains enough unbuilt housing tales to fill ten books like this.

After the First World War, for example, with the Council taking on responsibility for building homes, there was a big debate among the great and good as to whether or not council houses should have parlours. Some felt that a parlour was an unnecessary indulgence. Doubtless others among the great and good privately felt that having front rooms or sitting rooms would lead to the lower orders getting above themselves. For most developments, though, the parlours were indeed part of the house design, but in our parallel universe, there are to this day smaller homes in places like Sea Mills and Southmead.

Bristol's housing dearth after the Second World War was one of the worst in history. Hundreds of homes had been destroyed by German bombing, no new ones had been built for six years and the population was growing. The city took years to recover, and in the meantime the problem was so acute that almost 1,000 people took over empty military camps around the city as squatters.

The housing problem remained intractable for decades. In our parallel universe, the Conservatives come to power on the Council in 1973 and implement one of their election pledges; this was to commission 'shell houses'. These would have been half-built homes for cheap sale to young married couples to complete by themselves. At first, this looks like a hare-brained notion. But on second thoughts

... it's not completely mad, is it?

In terms of space, the biggest unbuilt project of recent years, which would have had the most dramatic effect of all on Bristol and surrounding areas, was the previous Labour government's 'Regional Spatial Strategy' (RSS). This basically stipulated that the four successor counties to Avon would have to find room for around 100,000 new homes by the mid-2020s.

That's 12 Bradley Stokes, three Baths, four Weston-super-Mares or two-thirds of a Bristol.

The RSS generated fierce opposition particularly in Bath & North East Somerset, North Somerset and South Gloucestershire. Residents worried about their views and house-prices joined forces with environmental campaigners who feared for the green belt. One of the very first actions of the Coalition government on coming to power in 2010 was to tear up every RSS in the country.

Nobody can predict when/if the Barrage or City's new stadium will be built, but you can be sure that housing will continue to be one of the most contentious issues in the area for decades to come.

It's altogether harder to forecast what the big spectacular unbuilt projects of the future will be. What will be the big buildings and infrastructure project which will be proposed, but will be stymied by expense and/or public protest and planning battles?

The list probably won't include shops and shopping centres; we're buying more things online these days. Maybe 3D printing technology, some of which is being pioneered in local universities, will reduce our shopping further. Cabot Circus, which was originally to be called Merchants' Quarter may prove to be the last major retail development ever built in Bristol.

Bristol's knowledge economy – information technology, bioscience, robotics, aerospace, nanotechnology and more – will certainly be important in the future. Partnerships between university researchers and private sector companies are already generating significant amounts of business and you could easily see how specialist research facilities will be proposed, but prove too expensive, or fall through when investors lose confidence in an economic downturn. It's perfectly possible that a big R&D facility might be prevented because locals fear biohazards, or toxic materials, or worry about military robots that might escape and mistake local residents for Her Majesty's enemies.

Bristol is a wealthier place than most other UK cities. A sizeable part of the population is educated, and making good money. These people will want leisure and entertainment facilities. There will certainly be planning issues over these. As the city continues to grow there will be planning battles over the way in which Bristol and Bath are fusing together along the A4.

But look also at the large numbers of Bristolians who are being left behind. With the numbers of unskilled and semi-skilled jobs in decline, and a state schooling system that is scandalously biased towards the middle classes, we are sleepwalking into the kind of social divisions that haven't been seen since Victorian times. If you want to be really dystopian, imagine proposals for a twenty-first-century workhouse, or maybe even some high-tech barrier fencing in a hapless underclass. It's not hard to write the script; the wall will protect 'hard-working' and 'law-abiding' citizens from 'crime and disorder'.

Science fiction? Of course, but flying machines,

robots and genetic modification were once science fiction, too.

To write science fiction, you don't need investors or funding. Your imagination has a limitless budget. To make big things happen in the real world requires a lot of cash. One of the reasons why Bristol reveres the memory of Brunel is that not only did he think big, but he was also capable of raising the money to make his big things happen.

While he was building the Great Western Railway between London and Bristol, it occurred to him that there was no need to stop at Bristol. You could create a modern transport link between London and New York, going via Bristol. The result was the ss *Great Western*, the ship that proved transatlantic steam navigation was practical, reliable and safe.

To link London and New York by the mid-twentieth century they didn't think in terms of ships, but of aircraft. That's why the ill-fated Bristol Brabazon was built, and then Concorde.

Perhaps in the twenty-first century people will dream of crossing the Atlantic with altogether different technologies. So let's finish with some more counterfactual history.

In 1972 the American science fiction author Harry Harrison (1925-2012) published *A Transatlantic Tunnel, Hurrah!*, a novel set in an alternate world in which Cabot had got to America before Columbus, and in which the American Revolution never happened (George Washington had been hanged as a traitor). America is still firmly in the British empire.

Now in the 1970s present-day, a descendant of Washington and a descendant of Brunel's are leading a massive project to link Britain and its distant colony by way of a tunnel under the Atlantic.

It's not a new idea. Jules Verne's son wrote a story about it in the 1880s. It crops up in several other science fiction stories, and there was even a 1935 British movie (*The Tunnel*) based on a pre-WW1 German novel. You can find it for free on the internet if you wish.

Perhaps a Transatlantic Tunnel – assuming it goes from Bristol, or somewhere near it – will be one of our great unbuilt projects of the twenty-first century. There are many ways in which it could be done. Engineers will tell you that it almost certainly wouldn't be bored through rock, but rather laid on the seabed, or perhaps suspended from the surface by pontoons. You can go online and read about existing or theoretical technologies that can shoot a train along such a tube at tremendous speeds. Technically it may be feasible; the big problem will be cost.

Nobody is seriously proposing such a thing at the moment, and perhaps nobody ever will. It may be that because of other technologies, or the shifting plates of the global economy, there will be no case for such an expensive undertaking. But if it is proposed, all you have to do is look at the history of, say, the Severn Barrage to predict that it won't happen soon and that if it ever does, it will probably be after several other schemes have failed or been rejected first.

ACKNOWLEDGEMENTS

Many people – journalists, historians, architects, archivists, librarians, publicists, developers, estate agents, engineers and more – have been extremely generous with their time and help. In many cases they've dived into drawers and attics to dig out long-forgotten material. Some have had to endure several annoying emails and phone calls seeking out recondite historical or technical details.

Any mistakes, of course, are entirely my fault.

Particular thanks are due to Adrian Andrews, Alex Dunn, Alf Perry, Andy Foyle, Andy King, Anne and Jerry Hicks, Anthony Beeson, Caroline Harris, Clive Burlton, Daniel Bennett, David Bell, David Innes Wilkin, David Mellor, Dawn Dyer, Frank Drake, Gerry Brooke, George Ferguson, Francis Greenacre, Karle Burford, Martin Rieser, Melanie Kelly, Mike Richards, Nick Henley, Nick Tyrrell, Nick Xylas, Paul Gough, Ravi Pandya, Simon Gurr, Tessa Coombes, Tony Dyer and many others whom I've forgotten. Especial thanks to the staff not already mentioned at the City Museum, M Shed, the Bristol Record Office and the Bristol Central Reference Library, without whom ...

Finally, extra particular thanks to John Sansom (who had the same idea) and Clara Hudson and Stephen Morris at Redcliffe Press for making it happen, and to Andrew Kelly and the Bristol Festival of Ideas for all their support. And of course to Monique for putting up with me (not just when I was doing this, I mean generally) and to Lauren for spotting the spelling mistakes.